Seasons in the Word

Liturgical Homilies

Year B

D0376169

Fr. John Sandell

THE LITURGICAL PRESS

Collegeville, Minnesota

www.litpress.org

1   2   3   4   5   6   7

Library of Congress Cataloging-in-Publication Data

Sandell, John, 1942–
    Seasons in the Word : liturgical homilies : year B / John Sandell.
        p. cm.
    ISBN 0-8146-2586-X (alk. paper)
    1. Church year sermons. 2. Catholic Church—Sermons. I. Title.

BX1756.A2 S26 2002
252'.6—dc21

2002067642

Contents

First Sunday of Advent   1

Second Sunday of Advent   3

Third Sunday of Advent   5

Fourth Sunday of Advent   7

Christmas   9

Holy Family   11

Mary, the Mother of God   13

Epiphany   15

Baptism of Christ   17

Second Sunday in Ordinary Time   19

Third Sunday in Ordinary Time   21

Presentation of Christ in the Temple   23

Fifth Sunday in Ordinary Time   25

Sixth Sunday in Ordinary Time   27

Seventh Sunday in Ordinary Time   29

Eighth Sunday in Ordinary Time   31

※ Contents ※

Ash Wednesday   33

First Sunday of Lent   35

Second Sunday of Lent   37

Third Sunday of Lent   39

Fourth Sunday of Lent   41

Fifth Sunday of Lent   43

Palm Sunday   45

Holy Thursday   47

Good Friday   49

Easter   51

Second Sunday of Easter   53

Third Sunday of Easter   55

Fourth Sunday of Easter   57

Fifth Sunday of Easter   59

Sixth Sunday of Easter   61

Feast of the Ascension   63

Seventh Sunday of Easter   65

Pentecost   67

Trinity Sunday   69

Body and Blood of Christ   71

Feast of Saints Peter and Paul   73

Fourteenth Sunday in Ordinary Time   75

Fifteenth Sunday in Ordinary Time   77

Sixteenth Sunday in Ordinary Time   79

Contents

Seventeenth Sunday in Ordinary Time   81

Eighteenth Sunday in Ordinary Time   83

Nineteenth Sunday in Ordinary Time   85

Twentieth Sunday in Ordinary Time   87

Twenty-First Sunday in Ordinary Time   89

Twenty-Second Sunday in Ordinary Time   91

Twenty-Third Sunday in Ordinary Time   93

Exaltation of the Holy Cross   95

Twenty-Fifth Sunday in Ordinary Time   97

Twenty-Sixth Sunday in Ordinary Time   99

Twenty-Seventh Sunday in Ordinary Time   101

Twenty-Eighth Sunday in Ordinary Time   103

Twenty-Ninth Sunday in Ordinary Time   105

Thirtieth Sunday in Ordinary Time   107

All Soul's Day   109

Dedication of the Basilica of St. John Lateran   111

Thirty-Third Sunday in Ordinary Time   113

Christ the King   115

First Sunday of Advent

There is a sense of warning to the words of Scripture this weekend. In the Gospel, the words of Christ, "Wake up, stay alert."

And in the words of Isaiah in the first reading, the lament of a people who had let themselves become too careless and self-satisfied, so that the only imagery left to describe the people was dried up leaves, blown away by the wind.

When the Hebrews had come out of the desert so many years before, they had done so with the clearest picture humankind had ever had of what it means to be God's people. An entirely new bond had been forged between themselves and God. A bond of hope, based not nearly so much on what they saw right there in front of them, but rather a hope based on what was promised, what was yet to be.

So a sense of incompleteness and an acceptance of it. That was part of the newness of revelation in the Old Testament. To be human meant to feel a kind of joyful hunger. Hunger because it was a real need and, until it was satisfied, no one could ever be complete. And joyful, because indeed it would be satisfied.

That joyful hunger is one that is easily lost. And when that happens—to a nation or a gathering of people or an individual—something in them dies. They lose purpose and resolve.

The words of Isaiah call to us today as surely and as clearly as they did to the Hebrews. Perhaps the best way for any of us to observe this season would be to make of it a time to re-awaken our awareness of just how deep is our need for the fulfillment that only God can offer.

And that must mean a firm resolve to purify our lives of anything that distracts us from that call, anything that dulls our spirit, makes us victims of the pressures of the moment.

I don't think it is too difficult to tell, really, when the spark has begun to dim, and we have begun to be frightened by our incompleteness, rather than called by it.

One such sign is a lack of patience with the natural pace of our lives. An unwillingness to wait confidently for our own growth, for God to fill up what we lack. Children rushing into situations and relationships years beyond their abilities. Adults impatient for success, working too hard, plunging themselves deeper into frustration.

Another such sign, I think, is the way we handle reversals in our lives. Do we experience these as disastrous? Or do we experience them as a natural element of our incompleteness?

So, waiting hopefully to be made full. An awareness of the fact that we are indeed dependent on God, and that it is good to be that way. As the Psalmist writes, "Lord, make us turn to You. Let us see Your face, and we shall be saved."

Second Sunday of Advent

It may be a little difficult to realize that this first reading is really a continuation of the passage from Isaiah begun last week. The tone of the reading has startlingly changed. Last week Isaiah was writing to a people in slavery, in exile, cut off from every security, every consolation they had known. But this week, Isaiah tells this broken people that even this is not too much to bear. Isaiah's words turn from a judgment to an assurance that the promise is still theirs, that God still has great things in store for those who believe in God, that the goodness, the joy in their lives is far from over, and that all they have to do is once again become a people who can look beyond what is happening around them, and look ahead to what they are called to be.

So there is something in motion in the universe, a motion toward newness, toward a wholeness, a perfection that we ourselves could not possibly imagine. And every set of circumstances, every situation in which we find ourselves—good, bad, pleasant, unpleasant—is meant to be a step forward in that inexorable movement toward wholeness.

But Isaiah is only the first of the three voices that lead us through this Advent season. Mark introduces John the Baptist very abruptly. He is the first figure in Mark's Gospel, the bridge between the Old and the New Testaments. Mark introduces him with a quote from Isaiah, to make precisely that point. The repentance, the change of heart to which John calls us, is the means by which the comfort promised by Isaiah will be ours. With the coming of Christ, the process of being made new has already begun within us. All we need do is recognize it, accept it, and clear the way of anything within us that may block that re-creation of wholeness in our lives. That is what repentance means. The word literally means, "Turn around." See what is happening. Be aware of what Christ has begun within you, and be a part of it.

The first line of this reading from Isaiah is one, I think, of the most eloquent in the Old Testament. Give comfort, speak tenderly to my people, tell them that their burdens will come to an end. So God charges the prophet Isaiah, and so God continues to charge the Church today. We are called to live our lives faithfully, patiently, without undue anxiety, without fear. There will be burdens to be borne, certainly, while we wait, but nothing that should terrify us, nothing that can possibly last more than a while. There could be no better meditation for us this Advent than this: "What we await are a new heaven and a new earth, where according to his promise, the justice of God will reside." So, make every effort to be found at peace in his sight.

Third Sunday of Advent

By now the Advent themes of remembering, of waiting, and of preparing are pretty familiar. But these readings today not only tell us that we are a people in waiting, they begin to give us an idea of what that waiting should feel like. And the words that are used to describe that experience are words like joy, peace, gratitude.

So the experience of waiting for the coming of Christ should not be one of frustration or emptiness. The Advent message is that, despite whatever setbacks we may experience in our lives, we must never let them destroy that fundamental joy, that fundamental gratitude for life that is so clearly the mark of a Christian.

Someone once wrote, "I think we all sin by needlessly disobeying the Apostolic call to rejoice as much as by anything else." In a world that is as often as not poised on the brink of self-destruction, it can seem that to rejoice, to be grateful for the gift of life, is a flight from reality. Most of what our culture calls happiness, from the complacent self-congratulation of those who consider themselves successful, to the boisterous escapism to be found in a wide range of diversions, most of what we tell ourselves is happiness is really just a thin imitation of the joyful state of mind that moved Isaiah to write in the first reading, "The Spirit of the Lord is upon me, God has anointed me to bring good news."

Far from being a flight from reality, the joy that marks God's people flows from the fact that they truly embrace reality. They understand the world and their place in it not simply in terms of their own experience, but rather in terms provided for them by the Creator of that world.

When Isaiah wrote this passage he was a slave, forced into service under the king of Babylon. There was certainly very little in Isaiah's experience about which to rejoice. But yet he did. Isaiah could see the purposeful hand of God moving and guiding His people even in this tragedy. And so can we. This is the truth about the world that believers can see when the Spirit of God is truly upon them. There is purpose, there is direction in the world, and there is nothing that can thwart that purpose or change that direction. To be a part of creation is reason for joy, because it is irresistibly being drawn toward God.

Isaiah's ecstatic vision of the future in the first reading is not an idle dream. We may not be able to immediately remove or overcome all of the obstacles which the world raises to such a vision, but we can surely outwait them. With time and with care, the growth will happen. We can be sure of that and rejoice in it. Because, as St. Paul puts it in today's reading, "He Who calls us is trustworthy. It will be done."

Fourth Sunday of Advent

The picture drawn for us in these scriptural passages is one of a God who moves, and who expects of his people that they move with him, that they follow God's lead. God doesn't sit back on top of a mountain and watch our lives with an amused disinterest. He leaps into our lives, shakes them. God's Word is a creative word, and that means that if we are open to it, it changes us.

This weekend's first reading pictures a point at which for the first time Israel had a capitol and a king who lived in a palace in a city, rather than in a camp in the desert. And the reading pictures King David as looking around at what he had built, and feeling a twinge of conscience. "It is not right," he says, "that I should have this strong safe palace, but that we should continue to worship God in the same dingy old tent we carried around with us in the desert. God too should settle down here. I will build a temple, big and strong and solid, so that everyone who sees it will know that this is where God is."

And that night, the reading tells us, God spoke to David through Nathan, and told him, "Just because you are ready to settle down, don't expect me to. Go ahead and build your temple. But don't expect me to stay there. I will be where I have always been, moving about in the tabernacles, the tents of my people, prodding them, calling them to get up and move." And the reading closes, really, with God's promise to David that God has yet one more tabernacle in which to dwell, for a time.

And of course that tabernacle was a human body. When Mary first became aware that Gabriel, "The power of God," was stirring up her life, her life was a very set thing. She was engaged to Joseph, and she fully expected to live out that life as a carpenter's wife, in a small village.

The words of Gabriel to Mary were not a command. Her freedom to choose was not lessened by the power of God. She could have said no.

But she said yes. And with that yes, she was changed, and so were we. From then and forever, a new openness to God, a new movement of God's power, was to be part of the human experience. That may be for us, as it was for her, a troubling thing from time to time. The answer that Gabriel will give when we express our concerns and fears and doubts, will be the answer he gave to Mary, the only one he ever gives. "Don't be concerned. Simply do as you are asked to do, and God will take care of the rest." The words of Mary in the Gospel must be our final Advent prayer, "Let it be done to me as You say."

Christmas

I don't suppose that in all of Scripture there is any truth that more surely reveals the reality of God's love for God's people and more powerfully gives shape even to humankind's most stumbling and uncertain response to that love, than does the fact that God speaks to us. Tonight Christians gather together to listen as the ancient story of Christmas is re-told . . . to proclaim their faith in the fact that it is true, that the God in whom we believe has spoken indeed, and speaks again, a Word of great power, the word Immanuel. He is "God with us," in us, of us.

What the opening paragraphs of the book of Genesis tell us was begun in the chaos and emptiness of the first moments of time, tonight the Gospel tells us was completed in the peace and stillness of a Bethlehem night. The Word became flesh. God chose to become like us, to take on the nature God created, and so establish between God and creation a bond so intense, so intimate that in it, everything is made new. The birth of Christ has literally re-created the world. It has made of the world a temple, the place where God has chosen to dwell. Because of the birth of Christ, not only is the world good and rich and beautiful, it is holy. It is a sacred place, and every human being who lives in it lives and moves in the sacred company of a chosen people. With the birth of Christ, human nature has become the tablets upon which the Word of God is written. Human nature has become the living Scripture that must make God known to God's people. The divine became human, and in its turn all that is human is called to become divine.

9

The Incarnation, once begun has never ceased, and never will. God's choice to take on human nature, human flesh and blood, mind and feelings, is as immediate now for us as it was in Bethlehem. The humanity Christ claims today is ours. The flesh and blood, the minds, the hearts Christ claims as his own body are those we see around us here, this moment. God's people must never simply celebrate the Incarnation. God's people must *be* the Incarnation. We must be, each of us, Christ in the flesh, for every other human being. Christmas is never simply a feast. It is a way of life, a way of life to which we have been clearly called, and powerfully made able to follow.

Christ must constantly be re-born in our midst, every day, every moment. In one of his epistles, St. Paul writes, "I live now not just I, but Christ lives in me." And that is the mystery of the Word truly made flesh. At Bethlehem, everything we are has been claimed by God, and drawn into the flow of God's own life. Now we are the voice by which God's Word is spoken.

Holy Family

It is simply and inescapably true that the family atmosphere, the family influence is the deepest and most formative element in a person's life. Psychologists tell us that by the time a child has reached the age of five or six, the basic value choices in life had already been made, and probably will not be changed. Some even say those choices are made by the age of two or three, perhaps even earlier. Decisions, perceptions such as "Is the world safe, or is it not? Are other people trustworthy, or are they not? Am I good and capable, or am I not? What do I respect, what is valuable to me, and what isn't?"

This feast emphasizes for us that it is in intimate companionship with other people, and only that way, that one becomes human, or at least what God means by human. It is by such intimate interaction that a person learns to be sensitive to the presence, the needs, the rights of other human beings. It is only in such interaction that a person comes to see oneself as an individual with one's own rights and one's own responsibilities. Simply enough, it is in such interaction that a person learns to love, and that is indeed something that must be learned. Once that has been learned, the answers to all of those fundamental questions change drastically.

That is true no matter how much the form of family life may change. The vastly increased mobility in our society, the high level of competition, specialization in jobs, means that family units of any kind break up much more quickly. Today it is almost the norm that by the time people are in their mid-twenties, they will probably be living hundreds, maybe thousands of miles away from their original family.

But the point is that no matter how the form of family living may change, the purpose remains the same. That is generating an atmosphere designed to promote the growth of sensitive, loving human beings, who know what it means to share their life with others, and who feel comfortable, willing to do so.

But all of that takes a real effort. I think one of the greatest challenges facing anyone who proposes to live in the company of others is simply to do that—to actively, pointedly, arrange one's life so that there is time for the gathering, for the family. When other concerns, no matter how noble, begin to leave no time to be with the family, then it is time to do some honest soul searching.

Let us treasure very carefully our family life. It is a valuable thing. It is meant, by God's design, to provide us with powers we desperately need. Christ spent thirty years of life doing just that, and that, every bit as much as his next three years, brought salvation. The Holy Family was no accident. Neither must be ours.

Mary, the Mother of God

Officially, the holiday that we are celebrating this morning is known as the Solemnity of Mary the Mother of God. But I suppose no matter what name is given in the missalettes, for most people January 1 will be just New Year's Day. A feast, a celebration of starting over, of new beginnings, new resolutions, a time when everybody's self-confidence is just a little bit stronger.

It seems to be part of our human nature that we are always willing, deep down, to believe that we can better ourselves, that no matter what our circumstances may be, growth, self-improvement is possible. All it takes is a good sense of resolution, and a little bit of will-power.

Really just that one idea, the idea that the world is basically a gracious place, and that constant renewal, new possibilities are characteristic of that world, apart from any other feast or title, just that idea is reason enough for celebration. It is reason enough even for worship, as we are doing this morning. It's a very Christian idea.

It's impossible, of course, to put the message of Christ into one paragraph. But if anything comes close, I suppose it would be the Beatitudes. Those really are the New Year's resolutions for God's people. To be peacemakers, to be patient, to be seekers after justice, to be merciful, to be seekers after holiness.

I think that points to the reason why the Solemnity of Mary really is a pretty appropriate emphasis to give our worship on New Year's Day. Mary's life was certainly characterized by as profound a knowledge of Christ, and more importantly, as close an intimacy with him, as any human being has ever known. And for us, just as for her, it is precisely that knowledge, that intimacy, that makes our growth, our self-improvement possible. The simple truth is that apart from Christ, our potential for self-improvement is very limited. Oh, we may well become better people, we may manage to make life a little more pleasant for ourselves, even for those around us, but that is about all. However, if we open ourselves to the call, to the presence of Christ, as did Mary, our possibilities become unimaginable, limitless. Our potential for growth becomes literally infinite. If we consciously and conscientiously give to our new beginning this first day of the year, the values, the direction that Christ brought to all of human life, there is nothing, not even death, that will be able to contain the powerful force for growth that will mark our lives.

Epiphany

The image of the life of faith as a journey is one of the most popular and powerful in all of Scripture. The image we celebrate today is that of the journey of the Magi, the three Wise Men. But it is a very particular kind of journey they make, one which serves well as an image of the life of faith. It is a search.

Unlike any other journey, to set out on a search means to leave behind something that is known, and move to something that is unknown. The Magi did so. In Babylon they were masters of their arts, their science. They were in control, at home. But they left that behind. They moved into unfamiliar settings, without even the security of knowing for sure what they would find there.

Well, so must a believer move. Starting out with what is known and familiar, one's own needs, one's own longings, one's own hopes, starting out from a world that is measurable and clear and obvious, and moving into a world that is infinite, and anything but obvious, moving into the presence of God, in order to have those needs fulfilled, those hopes realized.

A search is never planned. Certainly a searcher should be prudent, should prepare for whatever can be foreseen. But an honest searcher must be willing to be surprised, must surrender the right to determine their new experience in every detail. That is what makes it a search. The Magi came with questions, not with answers. They didn't know what they would find, how it would feel, what it would be. They had expectations, certainly, but not demands. They

15

expected to find a king. Had they demanded that a king be found in a castle, their search would have been fruitless.

So it must be with a believer. Those who are unwilling to be surprised, even disturbed by God, will miss God. Those who seek to move into God's presence, but only on their own terms, those who claim the right to define what God must be like, where God should be found, how it should feel to be in God's presence, those are no searchers. That, after all, is idolatry, it is to build god, not seek God out.

An honest searcher must be marked by a powerful trust. "What we will find, what we will become, will be good." I know it will be good, because I have been told it will be good. Told by one whose word I value, and that is enough to know.

In the lives of each of us, the birth of Christ has set in motion something very powerful, something very sacred. We don't know exactly what will lie at the end of that motion. But we have the Magi to follow. We will seek it out. And it will be of God.

Baptism of Christ

Each of the Gospel authors deal very briefly with Christ's baptism. It is almost as though they didn't really know what to say about it. After all, John's baptism was one of repentance for sin, and why the Messiah, the Christ should have undergone such a ritual must have been puzzling, perhaps even a little embarrassing for the apostles. The less said about it, the better.

All that Mark says about the actual baptism is that it happened. "Christ was baptized in the Jordan, by John." It is the few lines that follow, I think, that make his point. They are a clear and carefully constructed reference to the imagery used in the first few verses of the Old Testament, in the creation account. After he is baptized, Christ comes up out of the water, just as the land, the world, was drawn up out of the original watery chaos in the first act of creation. The Spirit descends, just as the Spirit is pictured as hovering over creation in the first account. But this new creation goes further than did the first. The sky is torn in two. Any barrier between heaven and earth is removed. This new creation is open to the Father, it is filled with the Spirit, and those who live there hear the voice of God.

So in Mark's account, Christ's reason for undergoing John's baptism might have been unclear, but the effect of it certainly is not. With the appearance of Christ, an utterly new bond between God and creation is begun, a bond centered, enfleshed, in Christ. This account presents Christ's credentials, introduces Christ as the Messiah. Not just a prophet, not just a miracle worker, but rather the Son of God, and everything else that would be said about Christ from then on would have to be understood in that light. From then on, wherever Christ goes, whatever he does, he does in the life of the Spirit, and with the power of God.

And it is that, I think, that underlies Mark's emphasis on the miracle stories. When Christ heals, it is the power of God literally re-creating the world, literally re-creating humankind, re-creating us, God's people.

I don't believe there is a better way for us to reflect on our own baptism than to use this first reading from the prophet Isaiah. It is God's own description of the mission on which God sends God's baptized. We are the servants whom God upholds, upon whom God has put the Spirit. Our mission is to move through the world gently, so gently, Isaiah writes, that we do not even break the grass on which we walk. God's world can never be forced into re-creation. And we are to move through the world confidently, effectively. The eyes of the blind will be opened, prisoners will be set free, and even the darkest dungeons will finally be broken.

Second Sunday in Ordinary Time

The figure of young Samuel, as he is disturbed from his rest, as he is called out by the voice of God, is the figure of us all. And too, like Samuel, we usually take a little while to recognize the call as being indeed the voice of God.

What we must learn to recognize is that God still does call each of us, clearly and directly. God is not silent in our age. He simply speaks with a different voice.

Actually, it was just a few weeks ago, on Christmas, that we celebrated the Incarnation, the fact that God has chosen to interrupt, to enter into our lives through the lives of other human beings. It is through what we hear from others, what we see of them, what we experience of them that each of us hears God's call, experiences God's grace.

And that fact is really a pretty reliable yardstick for us to use in measuring the success, the authenticity of our attempts to find God in our lives, to pick out which of the hundreds of voices we hear is really that of God.

That can all be put very concretely, I think. What do I actually do, in the course of a day, that is in any way of benefit to those around me? Are the human beings that people my circumstances better off because I am a part of those circumstances? I don't think it matters much what the benefit may be. It matters a great deal that it be. How do I experience the irritations, the nuisances of my human surroundings? As simply that, an irritation, no more, or do I give in, preoccupy myself with a noisy resentment, even anger, so noisy that I may even fail to hear in that irritation a call? To put it another way, how much do I insist that God's voice always sound like God, or better what I think God should sound like, before I will agree to listen? Perhaps, sometimes, the voice that we hear won't sound much like God. Perhaps it will sound like a complaining friend, a demanding co-worker, an upset or dissatisfied family member. Perhaps God's voice will sound like a seemingly foolish and limiting law or regulation, in the community, in civil society, in the Church. Perhaps God's voice will sound simply like the practical needs of daily living, the pressures simply of supporting one's self and one's dependents.

So, today, no less surely than before, God calls to God's people. And today, no less surely than before, we will hear that voice only if we are willing to recognize it for what it is. And the mark of our success will be how willing we are to accept God's call on God's terms, rather than on our own. Our willingness to simply say, "Here I am. I am listening. What do you want me to do?"

Third Sunday in Ordinary Time

There is to these readings a very real sense of expectation, of urgency, a sense that something incredible is about to happen.

In the Gospel passage, Mark pictures Christ's opening words as being almost an echo of Jonah's warning. "This is the time of fulfillment. The reign of God is at hand. Reform your lives, and believe in the Gospel." Jonah had a real "or else" tacked on to his prophecy. "Forty days," he said, "and if the city hasn't straightened up by then, it will be destroyed."

Christ's words, however, are not nearly so much a matter of saying, "Look what God is going to do to you," as they are a matter of saying, "Look what you are doing to yourself." We really don't need a prophet to walk up and down the streets to tell us that pride, greed, and hatred balance the world constantly on the brink of destruction. The disaster, the destruction that threatens humanity is not something sent by God. It is something we do to one another.

Well, if the danger of destruction arises not from some vast outside force, but from within human hearts, then so too does the hope of salvation. Christ's call to the coming of the kingdom is very clear. The reign of God will bloom where God has chosen to plant it. And with Christ, with Christmas, it was planted in us, in human lives. We are each of us agents, bearers of the kingdom of God. It will grow as we grow, as we begin to accept responsibility for our own personal growth, and that of our society.

Responsibility. To honestly recognize that each of us are the architects of our own growth. To realize that if we do live in Nineveh, in the shadow of destruction, it is because we have chosen to live there. We have put ourselves there. That is true for nations who choose not to feed and clothe and educate their people, who choose rather to be sure that they are capable of blowing up every living thing on earth, and it is just as true for individuals who experience their personal lives as empty, burdensome, even frightening. It is a fascinating thing to see that in the care of people struggling with emotional disturbance, the real moment of healing occurs when they realize that they are indeed responsible individuals, and quite capable of giving direction and purpose to their own lives. In our spiritual failings, too, that same moment is the moment of real grace, real absolution, forgiveness.

That is a moment that is difficult to reach. But if it is sometimes painful to look at our lives right now and have to say, "Did I do that?" it is a great consolation to look at the life of Christ, the kingdom of God made visible, and say, "I can do that."

Presentation of Christ in the Temple

The feast we celebrate this morning marks the observance by the Holy Family of the decree of the Law of Moses, the precept that the firstborn male offspring of everything alive, animal as well as human, was to be consecrated to the Lord, literally given to God. That was a very ancient precept, in place since the time of Moses.

In this, Joseph and Mary were simply acting in accord with what they were, faithful law-abiding Hebrews, devoted to the Law of Moses. Luke, the author of this passage, makes quite a point of the validity of the Law in order to make a point about Christ, who he is, and what he came to do. Because the next scene in this passage also flows from a precept of the Mosaic Law. It was that in any truth proposed, if two witnesses could be found to freely testify to the truth of the proposition, it was to held as true, by Law.

And so Luke presents two witnesses, Simeon and Anna. And the testimony they offer is that this child, Christ, is the one who is to come, the Messiah. What is being said is true, with the incontestable truth of the Law itself. Those who would reject Christ would be opposing themselves not simply to another self-proclaimed prophet, but to God's own will, God's own truth.

Luke was a physician, an observer of people, and he knew how human nature worked. He knew that faith was a difficult path, and that many would not take it. And so there is a darker side to this joyful ritual. Simeon says, "This child is destined to be the downfall as well as the rise of many. . . . He shall be opposed."

But not by all. Luke tempers the mood a bit with the second of the two witnesses. Anna. She is pictured as an old woman, one familiar with life, and its hardships and challenges as well as its satisfactions. So the virtues Anna would have brought with her to that meeting in the Temple would have been patience, years of it—faithfulness, self-discipline, and courage.

They were both brought to that place in the Temple, and there blessed with the Spirit of prophecy. Prophecy in the most classic Old Testament sense, the ability to see beneath the surface of the obvious, the ability to see, and to proclaim openly, what is really happening, in what seems to be the most commonplace, ordinary of events.

So, perhaps there is a sense in which it is true to say that prophecy is the first role of every believer. Perhaps we too are urged by a constant call to see beneath the surface, to read and to proclaim openly what is really happening in our lives. We are the people of the New Covenant, and in the testimony of our words, our lives, we too must proclaim the presence of Christ.

Fifth Sunday in Ordinary Time

This Gospel passage is one of very few references made to the human background of any of the apostles. At any rate Mark, with his love of detail, makes a point of describing how Christ walked across the room, took Peter's ailing mother-in-law by the hand, and helped her out of bed. He even adds that she immediately went back to work, waiting on her guests.

Toward the end of today's reading, Mark relates how in his casting out of the demons, Christ ordered them to be silent, because they knew who he was. Christ is often presented as making a point of keeping secret his mission as the Messiah. Mark especially makes the point that a lot of preparation would have to be done before the people would be ready, or even capable of accepting the reality of the kingship of Christ.

There would have to be a tremendous outpouring of human concern by Christ and his followers, an open acceptance of the unredeemed human condition, with all of its failings and shortcomings and suffering, and a ready willingness to do whatever could be done, whatever need be done, to ease that suffering, to make up for those shortcomings. When people began to see that such real love actually happened in the lives of real people, then they might be ready to listen to the Sermon on the Mount. They might even be ready to look up at the Crucifixion, and see there the most divine act of all: human suffering truly made God's own concern, and so human suffering made purposeful, bearable by human beings.

This is really the point of all the healing stories. It was not a matter of proving the divinity, or the power of Christ. Rather they were a matter of one person doing whatever was in his power to ease the suffering of another human being.

The first reading today is a passage from the book of Job, certainly one of Scripture's clearest images of a man for whom human living had become a burden almost beyond bearing. Job finally does make his peace with his hardship, as we all must, by opening himself to the fact that every aspect of life, good and bad, ultimately belongs to God, and not to us. That life can never be understood, it can merely be lived. Just that simple insight—our lives are God's, not our own—is the message for which Mark in his Gospel so strongly felt the need for preparation, a preparation that consisted of nothing more complicated than acts of caring for one another.

So, for us, too, today, as Christ continues to proclaim himself as the Messiah, that preparation must still be done. No one will believe that our lives are shaped by a gracious and loving God if we do not give them the chance to experience for themselves, by what we do, that grace, and that love.

Sixth Sunday in Ordinary Time

This first reading today is a few verses from the Old Testament book of Leviticus, one of the books of the Mosaic Law. And it lays out the process of diagnosing and quarantining cases of leprosy, a process that was followed not only among the Hebrews, but among many nations.

Leprosy was a fearsome disease, highly contagious, and fatal. And to separate the infected from the healthy no doubt did a good bit to control the spread of the disease. Still, there were a good many other diseases, even more fatal, more common, and more contagious than leprosy—tuberculosis, smallpox, etc. But people who suffered from these weren't made to cover their faces, wear a bell, leave the camp, and warn away anyone who might come near by yelling out their uncleanness. In the literature of so many cultures, leprosy was so uniquely despised, it was worse than contagious, even worse than fatal. . . . It was ugly. It was not easy to be compassionate toward a leper. It was much easier to be disgusted, to be repulsed.

I always think in this Gospel reading, that even before the leper was healed, Christ had worked his miracle, simply by reaching out and touching the man. In place of disgust, Christ put compassion. The real manifestation of God's power in this is not that one sick person is made healthy, but rather in the fact that a person universally held to be repulsive, unlovable, even evil, is in fact loved, is the object of God's mercy and compassion. And that is a miracle indeed. A miracle that heals not only leprosy, but heals as well human fear, human prejudice, human inability to love where and when the need is greatest.

Because of its ugliness, leprosy became for the Hebrews, and so many others, a symbol of everything that is ugly and frightening and evil. Human beings have always found a peculiar sort of satisfaction in lumping together all of their anxiety and fear and disgust, and destroying it, banishing it from camp, burying it. Thinkers over the years have even proposed that we can't really chase away the ugliness, because it is in us. What we really fear is ourselves, the ugliness, the weakness, the deformity that is in each of us.

So, as always, it is Christ who gathers up for us in himself all of these half-formed insights and gives them clear and forceful expression in the real lives of real people. That is how fear is overcome. That is how the broken and the weak are made whole and strong. The leper brought the dark and frightening side of his nature, and laid it out before Christ. And so for us. We must as confidently as the leper bring our fears and failings to Christ, and with the same words as his: "If you will it, you can heal me." Christ's answer will be for us as it was then: "Of course I will. Be healed."

Seventh Sunday in Ordinary Time

It is the very nature of God to create. Creativity is not something God does, it is something God is. So to be changed, to be renewed, to become more perfect is a sure certain sign of the presence of God. If this vital creative renewal ceases to be present in the Church and in its members, then we can say for certain that to some extent at least, we have withdrawn from the presence of God.

For Isaiah, in this first reading, the constant flux and newness of life was a consolation, a promise of growth and ultimate perfection. It happens not because we are the victims of whim or chance, but because we have been infused and surrounded by the presence of God that constantly rearranges and changes our lives. If we can see this in faith and trust, then even those things that we experience as injury rather than as growth can contribute to the final perfection of God's people.

Well, all of this is a lengthy way of making a pretty simple point. If we are to truly be God's people, we must reflect and express in ourselves the dynamic, creative life of God. We must do that as an institution, as a Church, as we must do it as individuals.

Institutional renewal, at least in a major way, faces us only infrequently. Much more constant is the challenge of personal renewal. It's a real danger sign when a person starts to feel that he is doing about as much as he can be expected to do, that he really has no need to pursue Christian growth much further and lets himself drift away from the instruments for personal renewal that God provides for all of us in His church, notably worship and penance.

Really, these readings today provide us with an early intro-duction to the season of Lent, a time that should be a period of very intense self-examination, very real renewal. How much of a place do I consciously carve out in my life for worship, and for reconciliation in the sacrament of penance? Life under the direc-tion of God must be marked by personal growth and renewal. Am I really open to that? Do I accept Christ's invitation to meet him in this sacrament gratefully and gladly? Today's Gospel shows how important the renewal of forgiveness was to Christ's mission. For him to say to the paralytic "your sins are forgiven" was a crime according to Mosaic Law. It was blasphemy, punishable by ston-ing, and it was one of the charges that resulted finally in his exe-cution. There was something dead in that society, in those people; an openness, an urge to grow that had died many years before. Christ faced that, and changed it, brought it back to life. So must we, wherever we encounter that kind of deadness, in our Church, our society, our families, or in ourselves.

Eighth Sunday in Ordinary Time

Over the first few decades after the resurrection and ascension of Christ, a fairly heated debate was held as to whether Christianity was an entirely new religion, or simply a new branch of Judaism. It is probably safe to say that the latter was the more commonly held opinion. After all, Judaism had branched off before, notably the Pharisees, Sadducees, and Essenes, while the central core, adherence to the Law of Moses, was retained by each branch. For so many centuries, however else they may have differed among themselves, the Hebrew people had faithfully held that salvation was possible only through the Law.

Paul was the most notable dissenter in all of that. His conversion experience had convinced him that Christianity was indeed, as he says in the second reading, a "new covenant," a law written not in books or on tablets of stone, but in the hearts of believers. Finally, some thirty years after Christ, Paul convinced the others at a gathering known as the First Council of Jerusalem, and the break with Judaism was complete.

And I think it must have been his reflection on the words of Christ such as those in the Gospel reading that solidified Paul in his position. In the image of the folly of putting new wine into old wineskins, Christ so clearly is saying that with him, something new was happening in the relationship between God and humankind and if that newness was to be realized in people's lives, it would demand a whole new mindset on the part of his followers. Some cherished old notions, values, would have to be abandoned.

31

For one, the idea that salvation could be found in the observance of a code of law and ritual, no matter how noble that code may be. Salvation was the work of God alone and accepting it was a matter of purifying one's heart, purifying one's love of God and of neighbor. Even more radical, "neighbor" meant everyone. All must be embraced and treated truly as what they are: the people of God, called by him, to him.

As we move into the season of Lent, what better time to reflect a bit on just how we ourselves sometimes still hang on to old skins, old ideas, old values, and so run the risk of losing everything. Do I believe that in service to others, I am obligated to do "my share," and no more? Do I believe that no one other than myself has any right to what I work so hard to earn? Do I believe that if I am offended I have the right to get even? Do I believe that worship that does not move me is not worth the trouble? These are old skins indeed, some of them as old as humankind. Until we rid ourselves of them, the new wine of Christ's love for all of his people may not take hold in us.

Ash Wednesday

In just a few moments we will come to the foot of the altar and signify again our readiness to take upon ourselves the observance of the Church's most intensely penitential season. And we will do that by marking ourselves with one of humankind's most ancient penitential symbols . . . the symbol of ashes.

They are eloquent things, these ashes we will wear. They call us to a readiness to at least try to see our lives as God sees them, to value in our lives what God does . . . and a readiness to at least try to purge our lives of everything that has been wasted and vain and foolish.

But so many times, the things that are wasted and vain and foolish in our lives are the things we hold dearest. How many anxious hours have we spent in concern over our material comfort? How graspingly do we hold to our pride . . . and for how many years, sometimes, do we let old hurts, whether they be real or imagined, prevent us from healing wounds in friendships, among family members? How destructively do we scratch for power, for control, in our relationships?

So not at all a simple thing, this purging of foolish vanity from our lives. The prophet Joel in today's first reading calls it a breaking of one's heart. This reading is part of a passage in which Joel recounts for the people the history of their salvation, how from the very beginning, God has worked in their lives. In everything that happened to them, his voice was there, urging them, leading them, calling them.

We too have a history of salvation. Look back over your life, from your earliest memory to the present. As you do, you will see that there is a pattern to God's love for each of us, in the major events, and in the everyday affairs. If you honestly reflect on all of that, you will see as did Joel that the history of salvation is a history of wavering faithfulness. You will see the times that sin has deafened you to the voice of God. You will see that just as there is a pattern to God's love, so too there is a pattern to our dullness, our sinfulness. So many times, as the prodding of the Holy Spirit has urged us to broaden the horizons of our lives, to become more than we are, so many times our own fear and pride and disorderly desire has narrowed our world, kept us rooted to the present, made us less than we ought to be.

For each of us this Lent, our challenge will be to recognize those patterns in ourselves, and to leave truly in ashes whatever has been sinful and weak and foolish in our salvation history. It can be done, and it can be done now. As St. Paul writes, "Now is the favorable time. This is the day of salvation."

First Sunday of Lent

Three days ago when we began this season of Lent, we did so to words, "Remember that you are dust, and to dust you will return."

So, at the heart of it, the first lenten insight that is offered us is simply the realization that we are in fact pilgrims now. That no matter how we experience our lives, however satisfying or frustrating they may be, they will change. A constant stream of renewal and rebirth is the plan that God has ordained for human life. We can ignore it, we can refuse to cooperate with it, but we cannot make it any less true. Sooner or later reality catches up with all of us, and we are changed whether we like it or not. So for us, for Christians, our challenge in this, as in everything else that we do, is to face reality, to accept it, to ourselves give direction and purpose to the changes that will inevitably mark our lives.

In the Gospel Christ says, "The reign of God is at hand. Reform your lives." The same idea is echoed later on, "Take up your cross and follow Me." The point is, you yourself take it up. Don't just sit back and let someone else lay it on you, as they surely will do. It is as though Christ is telling us that if it is claimed as one's own, even a cross need not be only a burden. It can be a crutch as well, if we choose to use it that way, a ladder to something greater.

In the life of Christ, we have been given any number of very valuable tools to use in this whole process. Voluntary, freely chosen penitential practice changes us. It prods our minds and our bodies and our spirit. It makes us aware of our fragility, of how dependent we can let ourselves become on the comforts that surround us. And it begins, at least, to lessen that dependence. Perhaps the first and most real value of penitential practice is also the most obvious. It makes us uncomfortable, less content with the here and now, and so detached from the here and now.

As we, like Christ, take what we are in our own hands and move into the desert, we too will be tempted. That is what happens in deserts. We will be tempted to put too much importance on all the wrong things, tempted to lose our perspective, our sense of balance. After all, that was the heart of Christ's own temptation. We will be tempted to irritability and impatience, to being judgmental and critical. In whatever sacrifice there is to be, we will be tempted to simply be victims, rather than priests; to be acted upon, rather than those who make the offering. Ashes may well be the remnants of what once was. But to a lenten people, they are also the seed of what will be.

Second Sunday of Lent

I don't suppose that there is much in life that human beings find more difficult to bear than a sense of being without purpose. It seems that people can do or endure practically anything, if they can do so with a sense that it means something, that there is a reason for it.

Because that is true, it is really not surprising that for most of us, our lives are given meaning by those moments when we somehow sort of see through all of the complexity and mystery of life, and, perhaps only for a moment, truly get the point, truly see the purpose behind all that we are asked to do and to bear. Such moments are truly revelation. Life is so much more than what it seems to be. There is at work in our lives a tremendous power, a power that is saving, re-creating the universe; a power whose presence is far beyond our ability to directly experience, but which nonetheless is so intimately bound up with even the smallest details of our lives, that in fact we are the agents of that power. That power is God's creative power that has been poured into our lives and is now at work within those lives.

Certainly for the apostles who witnessed the transfiguration it was a moment of just such revelation. It is as if they were allowed to see beyond their immediate experience, to see what was really happening there, the presence of God. They came away from that moment changed men.

The first reading pictures another such moment. At some point in his life, Abraham experienced his contact with God in such a

37

way that he felt compelled to respond with the sacrifice of his son. It wasn't until God intervened that Abraham realized he had been wrong, that what he had thought was happening was not. He wasn't being asked to satisfy God's anger or jealousy. Rather, he was being called by God to be the first step in what was to be a centuries-long process of revelation, a process in which God would slowly proclaim ownership of all of human life, all human effort.

So for us, as well. There is a great deal more going on in our lives than we suspect, a great deal more than we are capable of experiencing right now. We are all of us accomplishing a great deal more than we think in our everyday lives. All of the daily details of living have been charged with an infinite value, and that is true because our lives have been claimed by God, who consistently acts through our efforts, according to God's design. We cannot sense that presence anymore than could the apostles before the transfiguration. Like them, we can only trustingly abandon ourselves to the fact that it is there.

Third Sunday of Lent

The incident that is recorded in this reading from the Gospel of John is one of the few recorded by all four Gospels.

Unlike the others, however, John places all of this at the beginning of Christ's ministry. With the coming of Christ, in his presence, his mission, something new is happening. The relationship between God and God's people is being altered. Temple worship, in all of its details and prescriptions for every situation, just won't work anymore. The newness of Christianity was far more than just a change in buildings or ceremonies. Christianity is a change of heart, a new attitude, a new spirit, a whole new way of understanding God, and people, and the relationship between the two. Elsewhere in the Gospel, Christ tells the people, worship from now on must be in spirit and in truth. That is the avenue of the encounter between God and God's people. The real Temple from now on was Christ himself, literally his own body, and that of everyone who bears his name. So it was the emptiness, the uselessness, the silliness of the old forms that Christ overturned in this symbolic explosion. The idea that God could possibly be honored or impressed by a ceremony, when God can only be honored by a good life, by those who espouse God's values and live by them. The idea that sin can be countered, the justice of God appeased by a ceremony or sacrifice, or by any human act. Sin can only be countered by repentance and reconciliation, by that "change of heart."

Following that dramatic opening to Christ's life, time and again in the Gospels that same theme is repeated. It is not what goes on outside of a person that makes holiness; rather, it is what goes on in the heart. In Christ's own words, if there is some conflict, some unresolved, unforgiven hurt between you and another, go first to that person, before you come to the temple to worship. Until you do, or at least try, worship will not mean much. Don't be so quick to criticize what you see as the shortcomings of those around you. Look inside yourself. There is more than enough there to keep anyone of us busy.

So there probably isn't any better lenten image on which to base our reflection this week as this penitential season progresses. Cleansing the temple, making it new again, making it pure, simply getting rid of everything that has become pointless, empty of spirit and truth. That is precisely the purpose of penance, of self-discipline. That is what each of us must do in our own temple, our own lives.

So, living as a holy people should, that, and only that, is true worship. Anything that prevents or hampers that life is dead and useless. Once we have cleansed our lives of all such, we will each of us truly be the Father's dwelling place.

Fourth Sunday of Lent

In this first reading, the author is writing about the defeat of the Hebrews at the hands of the Babylonians. Jerusalem was destroyed, those who survived were deported to Babylon as slaves, and, the final degradation, Solomon's temple was burned.

As the historian writes about this terrible defeat, it is done so in a way that foreshadows Christ's sense of inevitability about his own death. In the mind of the author, it was not the power of Babylon that brought down Israel, but Israel's own sinfulness. So too with Christ. The Son of Man must be lifted up, because he chose to become human, to take on himself all of the human condition, including the effects of its sinfulness. And sin destroys human beings. Always, inevitably, inescapably.

Each time that we act selfishly, we become less capable of acting charitably. Each time that we turn inward, to our own concerns, we become less capable of turning out, to the world, to other people, to God. By eating away at the values upon which human life must be built, sin cripples us, so limits our ability to love that sooner or later we become incapable of living in God's world. Rather, we move into a world that we ourselves have created, a world utterly cut off from grace, from love, and from joy, a world marked by frustration, by a deep sense of failure, and finally by an eternal self-hatred. That, simply enough, is hell.

But if the effects of sin are inevitable for those who choose that, so too are the saving effects of grace for those who choose that. John pictures Christ as promising Nicodemus that it is the design of the Father that God's people be saved, move into God's company, and that the Father has pledged that design with the life of God's own Son. No one of us need ever be the least bit anxious or doubtful about what God has in store for our lives, what God intends for us. It is salvation, the fullness of human life, lived out in God's presence. The only concern any of us should ever have about our own success or failure as human beings is whether or not we want it, whether or not we will accept the Father's design, or set in its place one of our own.

Christ's words are a response to a question by Nicodemus. "Is God really with us? If so, how are we to know that?" Christ's response is, "God is with you because I am. Watch me. What you will see will seem like a crucifixion, it will look, it will feel, like death. But it will not be so. Everything that has been promised from the beginning is happening right now." Weakness is only weakness. It cannot last, and it cannot win. The Son of Man has been lifted up, and in that light, so have we.

Fifth Sunday of Lent

Right from the opening verses of John's Gospel he proclaims with a calm, serene certitude that Christ is the Son of God. He is God. For John, what the observer can see and hear is the least important dimension of what happened whenever Christ and humankind interacted. What really mattered was the interpretation Christ gave to each event, what it meant to him. Because through that, human beings could come to know what each event in their lives means to God, what is in his mind.

It is the perceptive eye of John's inspired faith that probes beneath the surface, and reveals for us what is really happening in the death of Christ. John so clearly sees that this is not simply a matter of a good man facing death. Rather, it is a matter of the infinitely creative power of God confronting face to face the weakness, the destructiveness of human nature. Since nothing that God touches can remain the same, John sees God again transforming the world and human experience . . . re-creating it. So that from then on, for those who follow Christ, even death was to become an experience of God's love, God's creative power. No longer a pointless waste, it was to become somehow sacred and valuable indeed. An old order was about to pass away, and something very new indeed was about to begin. In Christ's own words in today's Gospel, "Judgment is being passed" on the world as it is now, it is about to be changed. It is no accident that John records this insight immediately after Christ's explicit acceptance of his passion, and the Father's explicit affirmation of what was about to happen. Christ says, "Should I try to avoid this? This is why I came." Then he asks the Father to identify himself with his mission. "Glorify your name . . . ." John presents the Father's response as a voice from heaven, "I have done so, and shall again."

With that the divine transformation of the human condition, even human suffering, had begun. As Christ accepts what is in store for Him, the death of a human being had already begun to be a divine act, a rebirth into new life. Again, in Christ's words, "As it is for Me so it shall be for everyone. When I am lifted up from the earth, I will draw everyone to Myself."

As we have, I hope, begun to chip away at our dependence on satisfaction, on comfort, we should be freer than ever to see with John beneath the surface of what is going on around us, and be able to say with Christ that whatever dying to self we may have been able to accomplish this Lent has been far more than simply morbid breast-beating. It has been an act of divinely creative power, and by means of it, the old order, the old dependence, with its limitations and frustrations is indeed being overthrown.

Palm Sunday

This is a morning of great and powerful contrasts. In the Gospel passage with which we began this procession, there was a sense of triumph, a sense of something coming to a fullness, of moving in to where we are meant to be.

But there is an unsettling contrast struck, I think, by the fact that once the procession was over, we read the account of the Passion of Christ. At no other time of the year are we more explicitly conscious of ourselves as followers of a God, who values us, our discipleship, our faithfulness so highly that he paid for it with the life of his own Son. A strange sort of God indeed, who places himself so totally at the service of his people.

The frightening thing is that it was no unruly mob that finally caused, allowed the death of Christ. His death was a perfectly ordinary, perfectly legal execution. The kind of blindness, the dullness, the smallness of mind and heart that can crucify the Messiah is not some rare insanity in a few evil people. The flaw is much deeper than that. It is a part of our fallen nature. It is a mark even of people perfectly convinced that they are acting rightly, morally, justly. The frightening thing is that Christ was executed by good people. The cross and the palms were brought to him by the same hands. The great failing of the people is not that they were evil or bloodthirsty, but that they were complacent, equally ready to shout Hosanna, or crucify him.

That is the harshest image of all. The crowds. Those who did nothing, who simply stood on the edges of Holy Week, ready to stay and watch if anything interesting happens, but equally ready to move off if it doesn't.

Christ showed no anger toward those who waved the palms, and he showed no anger toward those who pounded in the nails. But elsewhere, in the words of John, he had this to say about those who simply stood on the edges of all those crowds. He said, "I know your deeds. I know you are neither hot nor cold. I wish you were one or the other, but you are not, and because of that I will spit you out of my mouth."

Those are terrible words. They are a terrible judgment on those who are always only a part of the crowd, too easily swayed, those who can be equally stimulated, entertained by Christ's triumph or by his execution.

This Holy Week must be a model for the months, the years to come for all of us. This morning we have moved in, in procession. On Thursday we will be invited to the Eucharist. On Friday we will again be reminded of the cross. On Sunday, if we do it all well and faithfully, we will be promised a life of new and resurrected holiness.

Holy Thursday

In just a moment I will go back to the altar and celebrate with you an ancient and timeless ritual. There will be created in this room a union between God and ourselves so intense and so intimate that it can be seen and felt and tasted. Acting with you, I will pick up a piece of bread and a cup of wine, and repeat the words that Christ used when he celebrated the Passover with his apostles for the final time: "this is my body" and "this is my blood." When I set them down again, an unthinkable act of divine power will have taken place. This room will have become an intensely holy place. The bread and the wine will have become the body and blood of Christ.

It's almost too simple really. The appearance of God in the midst of God's people should be more dramatic than that. There should be an explosion, a bolt of lightning, something. It just doesn't seem very God-like.

It must have been difficult for the apostles to avoid that kind of doubt as they lived through the first Holy Week. It must have been clear to them that Christ's mission was approaching a climax, that something was going to happen.

So as the apostles prepared to celebrate the Passover with Christ, they waited to see what he would do to finally proclaim his divinity. They must have been remembering the great miracles on that first Passover—the plagues on Egypt, the parting of the Red Sea, the victories of Moses over the armies of the Pharaoh. Surely Christ would choose something equally spectacular.

But what Christ did was give them bread and wine, and wash their feet. And when he had finished, he told his people, "Now you do this, do it in memory of me."

That was the proclamation of divinity that Christ had come to Jerusalem to make. It was not, certainly, what the apostles had expected. There must have been to them something a little bit foolish about the image of the creator washing the feet of his creatures. For some it was too foolish, and they left. Judas had hoped for more, and he left angrily, bitterly. But the others stayed, and they did what Christ asked them to do. They consecrated and shared the bread and the wine, and they cared for one another as Christ had cared for them.

So, in a few moments, when you come to take this bread, reflect on it. It looks so ordinary. It seems to be just a piece of bread. But it is not. It is the body of Christ. God is truly present here. And tomorrow, when you face the tasks and challenges and routines of life, reflect on them . . . they seem so ordinary. They may seem to be pointless, but they are not. They have been made new, they are the work of Christ. And God is truly present there.

Good Friday

This afternoon we have heard read the account of the passion of Christ. If we are repelled by the suffering of Christ, confused, even ashamed, it can be tempting to take refuge in the notion that somehow the passion had to happen, it was willed by God in accord with a design born in God's own mind, a design far beyond our ability to understand or appreciate. That is a tempting notion, because it is a comforting one. But it is not true. Christ did not choose to be crucified. Rather, he chose to be faithful, even if that meant to suffer and die. The simple fact is that Christ died because human beings freely chose to kill him.

There are any number of powerful figures in this account. The Pharisees, Peter, Judas, Pilate, Herod, James and John, Christ's closest friends. All of them had a part to play in the death of Christ. Some of them could have stopped it.

The Pharisees. To them, Christ was an impurity. He broke with Mosaic tradition. Nowhere is that more powerfully laid out than in the story of the Last Supper, the New Passover. I doubt that the Pharisees were evil. They were just complacent, self-satisfied. They had fallen into the trap of assuming that challenges only come from enemies.

Judas. More than likely he actually believed that his own vision should be Christ's, that he could manage Christ's mission, force a declaration of power by putting him on the spot. Very likely, Judas was a dedicated man, who had become too narrow, too caught up in his own vision. That is a deadly trap.

49

Even Peter, the Rock, knew a moment of panic and betrayal. It is much easier for us to understand what moved Peter. He was afraid. Fear does terrible things to people. It does terrible things to us.

Pilate. He intellectualizes, he debates . . . . What is truth? He tries to read and re-read the mood of the crowd. He weighs the release of Christ against the release of Barrabas. What is the interest of the emperor in all of this? So the last resort of a cautious politician: simply do nothing at all. I wash my hands of this. It is not my concern. At least this way I won't be hurt.

The cross was raised because no one stopped it. There have been too many crosses raised on too many hills. We call this day Good Friday. At least part of the goodness must be in our realization that it doesn't have to be that way. Our world need never be the kind of small and narrow, heartless thing that lets that happen. Let us challenge that heartlessness with the sure promise that two days from now we will again be called to live in a world as boundless as God's own power, as full of hope and possibility as resurrection must surely be.

Easter

If there ever was a time when human beings have been justified in repeating to one another the words of Christ' messenger at the door of the empty tomb, "Don't be afraid . . . you have nothing to fear," surely that time is now, tonight.

It is as though all of humankind's most perverted rage and fear had to be gathered up into one ultimate evil, in the most destructive act possible, to kill the Creator, to destroy the source of life, and by doing so, spend itself. Only God could have met that kind of challenge. Tonight we know that he did. Christ took on himself the concentrated fury of all of human sinfulness, the very worst that human folly could do, and it was not enough. The back of sin has been broken, and as long as we see the world in the light of this new fire, nothing can ever really terrify us again.

The resurrection is the heart of our faith. The foundation of it. Because the terrifying finality of death is seen to be a lie, we know that so much else the world holds to be true is also a lie. We know that truth is, after all, God's, and only God's Word can guarantee it. We know that the experience of the senses is a limited thing, and that we will never know the world as it really is, if we rely only on that, only on our own abilities.

The resurrection is the basis of our hope. It is the sure sign that God is true to God's promises. That for each of us there is infinitely more to come. We would be foolish indeed if we were to ever give in to the temptation to look around us and say, "This is what my life is, this and no more." God has great things in store for each of us, a great future. We can refuse to accept that future, but we can never destroy its possibility.

Finally, the resurrection urges us, excites us to love. To build between ourselves and our world a bond of concern, of involvement. We must never suppose that the divine work of Christ is a substitute for human effort. Quite the opposite, really. Christ's triumph over the power of sin, and the inevitability of human weakness demands of us that we ratify and reflect and imitate it in our own lives, actively, positively, not simply swept along on some imagined tide of grace, but rather by the freely conscious choices that we make.

A few moments ago, just outside the chapel door, we kindled a new fire, and we named that fire the "Light of Christ." We carried it through our midst, and we set it ahead of us. And we did so to the words, "Rejoice, exult all of creation. Christ has conquered, and darkness vanishes forever." That light can be challenged, it can be dimmed, but it can never go out.

Second Sunday of Easter

The picture of the early Church drawn for us in the Acts of the Apostles is one of a community with a deep understanding of its own reason for being. The early Christians were a people for whom life made sense. Not that their life was particularly easy—it certainly was not. Right from the start they were persecuted. But strange as it may sound to our ears, that didn't seem to matter all that much. They were a people who had found something important enough to give meaning and purpose to everything that entered into their lives, good and bad. They had managed to put together within themselves an attitude toward life that freed them from isolation, from pointlessness, and from fear.

So the Acts of the Apostles is a good book for us. It's good for us to dig around in it a bit, to try to understand a little better, to try to understand just what they had that we don't, or at least, that of which we don't have as much.

One of the obvious answers is size. It is easier for a small group to be cohesive, immediately responsive to one another's needs. Today Christianity is an immense organization, and it would be impossible for the Church today to structurally model itself after the gathering of the first Christians.

Another advantage that the early Church had over our institutions was a kind of temporal immediacy. A closeness in time to the events which generate the Church: the death and resurrection of Christ. The resurrection was the heart of their message. People who centered their lives around the resurrection were suddenly given a limitless world in which to live. Death became for them simply one in a series of stages in life, not in any sense the boundary of it. In a world that big, filled with that many wonders, persecution, even death, really weren't all that important. There were so many more important things to think about, to plan for.

So, the Church of those who saw Christ, and talked with him, those who knew him most intimately was a Church marked by a centeredness on the truth of the resurrection. And that truth generated in them a sense of excitement about their own future, a loving bond between one another, and a loving detachment from the passing concerns of secular society. Not because those concerns were particularly evil, but rather because they just weren't all that important. The people of the early Church lived in an infinitely big world, and they knew that they had an eternity in which to experience it, enjoy it all. That nurtured in them a sense of perspective, an awareness that nothing was worth sacrificing the way of life that would allow them to continue living in that world forever.

Third Sunday of Easter

This Gospel reading pictures what for Luke is the last in a series of appearances of Christ to his apostles after the resurrection. It is as though the point being made here is the summary, the most that can be said about all that had gone on.

I think there are two impressions left by the words of Christ in this reading. Christ is alive. That fundamental truth is really the heart and soul of our worship and our ethic. Christ is exactly who he was, what he was, before his death and resurrection. The events of those few days, events that by every imaginable human standard should have changed everything, in effect changed nothing. The mission of God's people is just exactly what it was: to see his presence, his dignity, his will enfleshed in a very human condition indeed. Christ's humanity is not something other than our own, not even in the light of the resurrection. Our covenant is not with a vague and shapeless God removed from our condition, but rather with a very real human being, one who bears visible scars, one who eats, drinks, sleeps, speaks with a very human voice. None of that has changed.

The second impression, I think, with which Christ must have wanted to leave his apostles is that no matter how puzzling, how contradictory, how unresolved our experience of Christ, no matter how little sense it may all seem to make from time to time, nevertheless everything is just about the way it should be. There is a point, a design, a purpose to everything that has happened, everything that will happen. It is as the Father has willed it should be, and that means it is right.

Christ's reassurance to the apostles certainly must have caught them at a time when contradiction was pretty much a fact of life. He had conquered death, and yet they were to die, probably under persecution. He had led them to freedom, and yet the most they were capable of doing was locking themselves in a room. He had claimed to be the Messiah, and yet they were still a subject people. In the face of all of that, to trustingly accept that the Father's design was moving toward fulfillment must have been an act of faith indeed.

So it is for us. When Christ touches us, it will be with a human hand; when he speaks to us, it will be with a human voice. That is where Christ has chosen to be, and nothing has changed that choice.

Perhaps the heart of an Easter faith is simply to accept that even crucifixion makes sense, and that, after all, it doesn't really change things much. Christ is now what he always was, what he has chosen to be. With us, of us. No matter what goes on around us, that has been the Father's plan from the beginning. And it will be completed.

Fourth Sunday of Easter

I doubt that there is anything more terrifying to a human being than even the suspicion, let alone the conviction, that he or she is alone in the universe, on one's own, set adrift in a pointless world.

So this revelation of Christ as the Good Shepherd is a welcome one. We are all in the hands of a God who knows us far better than we know ourselves, and who cares for us far more graciously and effectively than we could ever care for ourselves.

It was really just this insight that sparked the enthusiasm of the apostles in their earliest preaching. The kind of enthusiasm about the nearness of God that Peter reflects in the first reading. John and he had just finished healing a cripple, an act for which they had been literally arrested and forced to make an explanation. Peter's explanation is that there should be nothing surprising in that act of healing, because healing, wholeness must naturally flow into people's lives, as a consequence of a faithful awareness of the presence of God. In Peter's mind it would be impossible for us to be anything but whole in any area of our lives, if that faithful awareness is truly and humbly achieved.

This healing, shepherding power of God comes into our lives in really a wide variety of ways. First it comes directly from God. God reveals God's existence, that God is the Creator, that we are guests in God's world, living here for God's purposes. So, after all, the fact that some of the time we really cannot see very clearly the meaning and purpose of things that happen to us and around us is not very important.

God seeks to heal us through the life and death of Christ. God was not content to remain the Creator and Lord of human life. God wanted us to know firsthand that a life of faithfulness to God's call is an utterly unstoppable force. So God showed us, by becoming human, taking on all of our weakness and imperfections, even death, and showing in Christ's own body, Christ's own resurrection, how truly powerful the healing presence of God really is.

God seeks to heal us as well by surrounding us with a universe of created goodness. How many times have the care and goodness of God come into our lives through the actions of other people who have offered help, given us hope, offered patience, encouragement, any of a million kindnesses? When that happens, it is not by accident. It is a natural consequence of God's design, a design that makes each of us shepherds of one another.

So, let us truly seek out the shepherding, healing presence of God in our lives. In so many of the Gospel healing stories, Christ precedes the miracle by asking simply, "Do you want to be healed?" All we have to do is say, "Yes."

Fifth Sunday of Easter

There is something really very optimistic about the flavor of the liturgy this morning.

The Gospel reading, from John, speaks of the fruitful growth of the branches as long as they are connected to the center vine. But the Gospel says that we will bear fruit only if we are attached to the vine, only if we make it a point to be open to and accept the presence of Christ. We are attached to the vine, John says in the second reading, we are attuned to the presence of Christ through our belief in him and through our love for one another. Both are necessary, neither alone will bear fruit. Love gives substance, flesh and blood, to belief, and belief gives purpose and direction to love.

Belief and love. In Christian tradition the two are bound together in one word. Faith. For a Christian, faith, being attached to the vine, is not a virtue that determines only a relationship to God and a way of acting toward God. Beyond that, faith is a virtue that determines relationship with and behavior toward other people and toward oneself as well.

Certainly our reaction to God is an expression of our faith. The way that we act toward God is a reflection of what we believe to be true about God. If we believe God to be a stern and vengeful lawgiver, our attitude toward God will be largely one of fear. If we believe God to be some sort of vast impersonal cosmic force, out there somewhere among the stars, our attitude, in the midst of daily living, will probably be something like, "So what?" But if our faith is formed rather by what God has revealed about himself, in

59

the story of the prodigal son, for example, then our attitude will be one of humble, grateful acceptance of all of the unearned goodness we have received.

Faith gives us a new insight, a new understanding of the people around us as well. In faith we see that every human being ever created was created in God's image, and that every person ever created is deserving of our acceptance, our love, our service.

Our faith determines too our attitude toward ourselves. If we are truly aware of our connection to the vine, then self-respect, a healthy self-love, is a natural and easy thing. If we can honestly see and accept ourselves as instruments of Christ's life in the world, then somehow the personal standards of society seem pretty vain and empty, and truly living out the personal standards of Christ becomes something we owe ourselves.

Truly there is cause for optimism. The vine is growing, and the branches will bear fruit.

Sixth Sunday of Easter

The first fruit of the paschal mystery is that the reality of God is described to God's people not in terms of some external power that forces itself in on a person, but rather in terms of an inner state, something that happens inside of a believer.

The words that are used by John to speak of all of this are *love* and *joy;* it is John who tells us what love is. According to the second reading: "Love consists in this, in that God has loved us, and sent his Son as an offering for us." So, most simply put, love is what Christ has done for us. That is what we must do for one another, in every situation in which we find ourselves.

The first thing that Christ did for us was to give himself. He did so freely, with full awareness of all of the implications of that choice. And so must we. If our relationship with others is genuinely loving, we walk into it with our eyes wide open.

Just as Christ did for us, love must mean accepting a certain amount of responsibility for the welfare of others. Recognizing that, to a certain extent, what is good for the other I must consider as good for me as well.

I say "to a certain extent" because real lovers never try to substitute their own virtue or ability for that of the other. Rather, a true lover assists others in engineering their own growth, exercising their own virtue and ability; a true lover demands of others that they become the best they can be.

Once that demand is made, a true lover steps back and allows it to happen. I suppose it is at this point that the quality of

love is most sorely tested, the point at which control is freely sur-
rendered: willingness to let the circumstances of our lives strip
us of power, of control.

Finally, in his Gospel, John gives us one of the surest sign-
posts to use in judging whether or not all of this is happening.
The word he uses is *joy.* In Christ's words, "I have done all of this,
and you must do it too, so that your joy may be complete." That
is the mark of a lover, the mark a Christian lover: joy.

I think joy means a basic sense of rightness about one's life.
To go beyond the experience of the moment and say, "Even though
it may not feel like it from time to time, things are going about as
they should. Even if I have to grapple from time to time with problems, they are real problems, and working to find a solution to
them will mean real growth."

So, God has indeed loved us, and sent us to love one another.
In the face of that the only possible response is joy.

Feast of the Ascension

Today we celebrate an event which begins to introduce our time in the history of salvation. A great change was made in the way that God is present among God's people. Not the end of that presence, by any matter of means, but a change in the way that presence is experienced, what it feels like.

The first reading today speaks of this pretty clearly. Christ cautions the apostles to wait before they set out on the mission he had given them, the mission of spreading God's word, God's personality to everyone. "Wait in Jerusalem," Christ says, "until I send the Spirit, before you set out." In effect he is saying, "Don't try to do all these things on your own. Wait till I can be with you. On your own, you will only mess things up." A pretty good indication of how true this is is given in the next line, where the apostles are pictured asking, "Is this the time, Lord, when you will restore the kingdom to Israel?" Even after all the time they had spent with Christ, they had still pretty well missed the point of what he had to say. They still halfway expected Christ to lead an army against Rome and bring back to Israel the glory of the good old days under Solomon. Christ's answer to them is about the same as it always had been to such questions. He cannot say yes, because such a kingdom is not his concern, and he does not say no, because there certainly is a kingdom yet to come. So He says something like, "You'll find out. The Spirit who is to come will teach you everything. Under his guidance you will build my kingdom."

But there is a further revelation to be drawn from this event. Nothing that Christ ever did or said was meant for him alone. Christ did not speak to himself. In revealing to us what he is, Christ also reveals to us something about ourselves. The ascension is a description of our own future, of what lies in store for us. It is a repetition of the promise given at Easter that a life of fidelity to the Father is a life that simply does not end. In the words of Christ just prior to the ascension, we human beings have been given the task of taking up his saving role, and at Pentecost we are given the ability to carry it out. If we make use of that ability, we have every right to rejoice today, not only because of the glory that has been given to Christ, but also because of the glory that waits for us. The ascension is Christ's last word of encouragement, his way of saying, "Be faithful. There are a good many things yet to come."

Seventh Sunday of Easter

Over the past few weeks a lot of attention has been given to the Acts of the Apostles, the book from which this first reading today is taken. It is a fascinating book, really: part history, part catechism, part homily.

The Church was founded with a very real purpose, and the early Christians experienced themselves as stewards of a very strong sense of identity. They knew with a real certainty that there was a difference between them and everyone else.

They were a holy people, set apart by and for God. Christian holiness consists first in our awareness that each of us, as individuals, have been personally called into the presence of God. The experience, the awareness of just that, the nearness of God in our lives—collectively as a Church and personally as individuals—has for two thousand years been the driving force behind every step forward that Christianity has made.

And nowhere is that more clearly expressed than in today's Gospel reading. In this discourse, Christ is most intensely aware of his unity with the Father. Like every human being—and Christ was most certainly human—he had moments of greater and lesser clarity in his awareness of the nearness of God. But for now there was no doubt in his mind. Every word in this passage reflects the intensity of Christ's experience of being at one with the Father, and every word reflects too the effect that this experience had on him. His words are filled with a kind of quiet elation, a calm self-confidence, a sense of purpose. Perhaps most important, there is no hint at all in anything he says in this discourse, no hint of blotting out his awareness of the problems and trials that were certainly to come for him and for his followers. There is no pulling back from the harsher realities of the world. Rather, his attitude is that, in spite of all the harshness, there is a basic rightness to what life would hold for him, a rightness that made any notion of escape, of dropping out, really unthinkable. God's presence made Christ aware of the fact that no matter what happened to him, it was good to be there. Christ's prayer in this passage is that the apostles achieve that same attitude, that they too somehow manage to attain this sense of rightness about life that is such a clear mark of the presence of God.

We are all called to share in this experience. Holiness must be the lifestyle, the self-image of every Christian, a holiness that is based on our own personal awareness of our intimacy with God. The state of mind of Christ in this Gospel reading, the calm, confident, joyful acceptance of one's lot in life, is not reserved to Christ or to a few mystics. It is offered to each of us.

Pentecost

In the first reading, the picture that Luke draws of the apostles gathered together after the resurrection is of a pretty confused and frightened group of men. They knew they had a mission to preach the Gospel, to somehow reproduce for others the experience they themselves had had of Christ. But there was still that huge gap between knowing and doing. They had insight, they had understanding, they even had faith. But they were still missing that mysterious quality that makes the difference between one who simply knows God's word and one who lives it. No one can say really very clearly what it is. We can only say when it is there. It is an elusive mixture of confidence, both in God and in oneself, and zeal, what the Beatitudes call a hunger for truth and righteousness. And perhaps more than anything else, it is simply courage. Courage doesn't mean not being afraid, only a fool is that. Rather, courage means not trusting one's fears, not letting them take control of one's life. It means acting in spite of fears and doubts and insecurities.

An unlikely group, certainly, and left to themselves they would not have been very effective. But the great truth of this feast is that they were not left to themselves. God made up for human failing. God gave them the confidence, the zeal, the courage they needed. God gave them the Holy Spirit, God's own life force, and they became indeed not merely hearers of the word, but doers.

Just as the Holy Spirit prodded the apostles out of their fear, so too does the Spirit prod us. Our challenge is really the same:

the challenge to realize that all of human life, every facet of it, has been infused with the powerful presence of the Spirit. And because of that, the challenge to realize that all of human life, the good that we do, the evil we endure, is a divine mystery. The fact is that because of Pentecost, human life is as far beyond our understanding as is divine life. That means that there is only one way to realistically affirm our lives, and that is with faith, as believers.

As believers, we know that there may very well be no immediately obvious connection between what we are asked by the Spirit to do and the good to be derived from doing it. As believers, it just doesn't matter very much whether or not that connection is obvious. We know that it is there.

So, following the second reading today, we prayed the very ancient sequence "Come Holy Spirit." For two thousand years that has been the Church's constant prayer. The Spirit's answer is simple. "I am here. I have always been here." So the Spirit has. The life of each of us is a constant Pentecost. In everything we do, we are the Spirit's dwelling place.

Trinity Sunday

At the heart of it, our religion is a mystery, both in revelation, on God's part, and in our faith response. Neither God's action nor our own can ever be satisfactorily laid out in logical, reasonably proven formulas.

Well, I suppose there is no truth of the faith more aptly described as mystery than that on which the liturgy asks us to reflect this morning, the truth of the Trinity. Three persons in one God, one divine nature . . . Father, Son, and Holy Spirit.

The mystery of the Trinity is really the heart of what God reveals to us. Anyone who hopes to approach God as God really is must approach him as Trinity, as three in one. We must respond to God as Trinity as well.

The threeness of God is more than just three different roles played out by the one Being. God would have always been perfectly the Father, the Creator, even if God had never reentered the world as the redeemer. God would have always been perfectly the Son, who re-created the world in God's image, even if the Son had never agreed to stick around as sustainer, supporter of life, in the Spirit.

In the Father, God perfectly manifests the qualities of power, creation, life-giving, the qualities of majesty and transcendence, the otherness of God. That calls from us a response of awe, of acceptance, of obedience, of humility, a tinge of what we used to call the "fear of the Lord." Fear in the sense of a healthy respect for the fact that our lives are in God's hands, that God's power is unassailable, and that to reject God is inevitably self-destructive.

In the Son, God perfectly manifests the qualities of Redeemer, as one who has allowed himself to be formed by the Father, the qualities of infinite fidelity, of perseverance, self-giving, the qualities of unhesitating forgiveness, and universal peoplehood, without compromise or exception. The Son became like us precisely to show us what people formed by the Father must be. So if our faith is to be truly God-centered, we too must be faithful, unhesitatingly forgiving . . . we too must persevere as servants of one another, without exception or compromise.

Finally, as the Spirit, God binds together the Father, the Son, and humankind into an eternal community. It is true to say that we are constantly re-made by the indwelling of the Holy Spirit, that when the Father looks at us, God sees the Son. Pentecost is the final fulfillment of the ancient promise in the book of Genesis that speaks of God creating us in His own image and likeness. God has created us, has redeemed us, and has bound himself to us for all eternity. God has made himself known as Father, Son, and Spirit. God has named himself at the same time One and Many. And it is in that name that we believe.

Body and Blood of Christ

Today we recognize and celebrate the fact that the presence of God with us is to be found in a very tangible, material way. Christ's presence to his people is a total one, in body as well as in Spirit.

Judging from passages such as the Gospel for today, the Eucharist, along with the forgiveness of sin, seems to be one of the few sacramental rites as we celebrate them today, clearly, unmistakably celebrated by Christ himself, in just about the same way as do we. The story of the multiplication of the loaves was from the beginning used as a symbol of the Eucharist.

St. Paul's earliest concern was that the pure and authentic reception of the Eucharist not be marred by any other squabbles and disagreements among the early churches. Eucharistic worship must be a bond of unity that goes beyond every barrier that human beings erect between themselves and others, barriers of politics, economics, race, even of religion. That means that to honestly take part in the Eucharist is to say, and try to mean, wish to mean, that there is simply no human being anywhere whom I can rightly consider my enemy.

For thousands of years, even before Christianity, any number of religious insights, ethical systems, have urged and expressed a love of one's neighbor, one's friends. But only the Eucharist expresses, demands, a love of one's enemies, even to the extent that word itself, "enemy," must be drained of meaning.

If we are to follow Christ, we must see ourselves as called to offer our love, our service, our self-giving not only to those with whom our lives are immediately, experientially bound up. We must be ready to offer all of that as well to people who have no measurable claim on us at all, people who have done me no service, brought no good into my life, people with whom I am related in no measurable way.

That is true, but it is not true enough. Far beyond those who have done us no good, we are called to love, serve, care for those who have done us harm, and who in all likelihood will do so again given half a chance. It is those with whom we are called to take the Eucharist.

So, God has chosen to live with the people. God has chosen to live with us as we are. We are not pure spirits. We are physical, material creatures. Christ has chosen to make his presence with us physical, tangible, so that we might see ourselves called to do the same. Our community is truly eucharistic when Christ's presence is made truly physical, through our own . . . when the people who move through the sphere of our presence—here, now, today—experience Christ's own radical, tangible, physical love. The Eucharist, after all, is not only a gift given to us by God. It is a gift we must give to one another.

Feast of Saints Peter and Paul

As believers, we accept and rejoice in the fact that Christ is the founder of our Church. But it is equally important to keep in mind that this gathering of believers, so divine in its origin, is very human in its form. Our faith is shaped not only from within us by the grace of God, but from without as well, by the simple force of personality of men and women who have permanently imprinted this way of life, with the effects of their own very personal, very human strengths and weaknesses.

St. Peter and St. Paul are important to you and me precisely because Peter and Paul were no different from you and from me. Christ chose to put the Church in the hands of perfectly ordinary people, and perfectly ordinary people have built that Church, nurtured it, and brought it to us two thousand years later.

They were about as unlike as two people could possibly be. Peter seems a sort of a bulldog type, a hard-working, simple man of simple virtues. A family man, with strong family loyalties. Very impulsive—a couple of times he speaks before he thinks, and then regrets it.

Paul was intellectually brilliant, nothing simple about him at all. Tremendously energetic in causes that gripped him; totally disinterested in those that did not. He was impatient, even sarcastic, with people who were not as sharp as he. And yet even though so different, Peter and Paul worked together very well. Peter had a strength and a gentleness that gave stability and direction to the restless brilliance of Paul. And Paul prevented Peter from just sitting still and going nowhere.

Peter, of course, knew Christ as a Jew. Peter, at first, did not see Christianity as a new Church, but rather as a reform movement within Judaism. Peter believed that the efforts of the apostles should be limited to Jews, and if any non-Jews wanted to follow Christ, they would first have to convert and follow the whole complicated Mosaic Law.

But Paul knew that that wouldn't work. He saw Christianity as a totally new plan of salvation, open to everyone, Jew and non-Jew alike. Paul saw the old laws as shackles that must be cast. The whole thing was finally brought to the bishops in the first Council of Jerusalem, and Paul carried the day. Peter eventually became himself an outspoken apostle to the Gentiles, ending up, like Paul, in Rome.

So Peter and Paul. Both strong, capable, holy men pursuing the same goal from widely differing points of view, and yet neither of them feeling any need to condemn or exclude the other. The lives of Peter and Paul are an invitation to us to respond more fully, more humanly to our common vocation to live in the Church. And those lives are an assurance that people, people just like us, can do that. The only real way to venerate the saints is to imitate them.

Fourteenth Sunday
in Ordinary Time

In a series of images which in a real way concludes with this Gospel passage, Mark summarizes Christ's presentation of himself to the people. It began with the parables of the kingdom, and then in a series of four miracle stories—the calming of the storm, the casting out of a demon, the healing of the woman, and the raising to life of the little girl—Christ's presentation of the fact that in him indeed all power in heaven and earth has been settled by the Father. Power enough, more than enough, to bring about the coming of the kingdom, make it real.

Scattered throughout all of this there are descriptions as well of the response of the people, a wide range of response. There is amazement, there is doubt, there is awe, there is fear, there is ridicule, and, occasionally, there is faith.

In all of this a very strange image begins to emerge. The one who makes that magnificent promise, the promise of a new creation, a new kingdom, the one who claims and exercises all power over that creation, presents himself as very much an ordinary person, an ordinary person who asks of us in response pretty much what any other ordinary person asks of us: our trust, our acceptance, our affection, our patience, our fidelity. It is that, the Gospel teaches, that will bring the promise of the kingdom to full fruit and unleash the re-creative power of Christ in the lives of his people.

The problem with all of that, as we so often see it, is that it just doesn't seem very God-like. No one who claims what Christ claims should be quite that ordinary, quite that . . . human.

To the people pictured in this Gospel reading this morning, Christ was probably especially ordinary. They had watched him grow up, they knew his family. They had known him when he was a little kid. They had watched him wrestle with the idea of his own mission, grow restless in his father's carpenter shop, and finally pick up and leave home, following his own design. Pretty ordinary stuff, the stuff of human experience. Nothing very Messianic, divine, about this guy. The Gospel says, "they found him too much for them." Actually, that doesn't seem a very good way to put it. Better would be, "They found him not nearly enough."

Well, so too for us. It is precisely there, in the exercise of all of the virtues of ordinary human relationships, in trust, in acceptance, in affection, in patience, in fidelity, that we too will experience the building of the kingdom, the power of Christ. There is in this truth a real consolation for us, a sense of purpose. Because no matter how the circumstances of my life may seem, if I am living them well, then what is really going on is Christ's own mission, his own life. And through my ordinary virtue, the world is being remade.

Fifteenth Sunday in Ordinary Time

Usually the word "prophet" makes us think of one of two types of figures. Either we picture someone like John the Baptist or Jeremiah or Jonah, the kind of fiery, intense reformer, whose purpose seems to be to constantly call attention to society's shortcomings. Or we picture an Ezekiel or Isaiah, a mystic, someone who can look at the world, even into the future, and read truths unavailable to the rest of us.

But the gift of prophecy is not limited to them. In the second reading St. Paul says that every one of us has been given the ability to grasp and appreciate and express the plan which the Father has for the development of human society. Simply enough, that is what prophecy is all about.

Scripturally, the word "prophet" means one who speaks the mind of God. All of those who recognize in the life of Christ a standard for their own lives, and accept that standard, become a prophet, become called to represent to the world the values, the attitudes, the understanding that shape a life in accord with the mind of God.

That means that there may be times in the lives of each of us when our call to prophesy, to speak the mind of God, will demand of us that we take a stand that is critical of society, that will set us at odds with society . . . the stance of a reformer, the stance of a modern-day John the Baptist or Jonah or Jeremiah.

It may be too that at times our call to prophesy will ask us to take the stance of an Isaiah or Ezekiel, the mystics who set aside the familiar and dependable tools of reason and logic so as to free themselves to base their lives on the deeper truths that make up the mind of God. It is a prophetic act to recognize and to proclaim that all of life is ultimately mysterious, and that the most we can ever really grasp is the surface of it, what appears to be. We are all of us, time and again, called to live comfortably, gratefully, joyfully, in a world that is very often unreasonable, uncontrollable, and mysterious.

The point is that for each of us the exercise of our call to prophecy will be as varied as is the need of God's people to know the truth, and there is no situation in which that need is not a real one. At work, in school, in community, at recreation, there is a way of acting, understanding, relating to others that is in accord with the Christian call, with God's plan for human activity, and there are ways which are not. All of us, in each of these situations, are called and sent to act out with all of our ability, the way that is.

Sixteenth Sunday in Ordinary Time

One of the most common literary devices used by the Old Testament prophets is the kind of thing of which this first reading today is a good example. And that is to draw a picture of the great contrast between the way things are now and the way they will be sometime in the future.

It was to be a Messianic age, brought about by God's own agent, the Messiah, the Anointed One, in God's own time. And all the people had to do, really all they could do, was to wait, patiently and faithfully, for God to move.

Then, of course, God did move. God sent Christ, with the message that that renewed and perfect world that had been promised for so long was not going to be just the handiwork of God. God had become human, and from then on, humanity was the agent God had chosen, through which God would accomplish God's work.

Well, that is a staggering challenge. It calls for some very concrete virtues. It calls for faithfulness, for patience, for a great deal of humility. And perhaps as much as anything else, it calls for balance.

One of the most obvious applications of all of this is found in the Gospel reading for this weekend. Finding a balance in one's life between action and rest, work and play, service and prayer. Even Christ said to the apostles from time to time, enough is enough, slow down, come away and rest, and think for a while. We don't do that very well as a culture. We are not good relaxers. Too many times our play, even our prayer, is as driven and draining and anxious as our work, and that is not good. Those who are never genuinely playful, genuinely at rest, are not balanced people, and their chances of contributing to their own perfection, let alone that of the world, are pretty slim.

There is another dimension to the virtuously balanced personality, and that is a moderation in the expectations that we set up of ourselves and of one another. The fact is that in a world that grows perfect only slowly, every inhabitant is still imperfect. Now that can never mean that we let ourselves grow passive in our judgment of evil as evil, but it does mean that we never grow too discouraged in the pursuit of good, even though that good may have to co-exist with evil for a time.

So, a balanced personality, always tempered and guided by faith. A personality that is open to all of the potential goodness of life, but one which is prudent enough to be able to concentrate on those goods which are under one's control, which can be accomplished, even if it doesn't seem like much. That is the messianic role of every one of God's people. That is the way, it is the only way, that the world will be made perfect.

Seventeenth Sunday in Ordinary Time

One of my favorite figures in this Gospel reading is the little boy who contributed the original five loaves and two fishes. We can almost picture him sort of looking around and thinking something like, "It's too bad, really, about all these others. I wish there was something I could do. But five hunks of bread are just five hunks of bread. My little efforts aren't going to change this mess one bit." Then suddenly there are a couple of apostles towering over him, saying, "Yes, there is something you can do. Give your bread and your fish to Christ." The kid says, "This little bit?" The apostles reply, "Yup. That little bit."

Well, the point is clear. If that child had insisted on being his own judge as to what the effects of his efforts could reasonably be expected to be, then he would not have made that effort, and an awful lot of hungry people would have sat there for quite a while. But he didn't. He was content to simply make the effort and let Christ be the architect of its effects.

There is a very profound truth in all of this: those who live in God's world never know the final outcome, the full effects of their efforts. That is so because it is, in fact, God's world. It is God who builds it, and by God's choice part of the essential raw material of that building is the effort that we make. That means that there is a real sense in which God depends, in the building of the kingdom, on the efforts that we make to be virtuous.

Just think of all the times in the course of our lives that each of us is asked to make an effort at virtue. An effort which may not seem to pay off at all. The times we are asked to be charitable to someone whom we know is going to try to take advantage of us. The times we are asked to forgive someone whom we know is going to hurt us again. The endless demands on patience that are made of those who live in the company of other human beings, even though it never seems to be enough. Every Christian, sooner or later, has to ask, "Is it really worth it? If I do give up my personal five loaves and two fishes, is anything good going to come of it?"

Christian tradition answers that with an insistent clarity: "Yes. It certainly is worth it. Something good will come of it." To the next question, "Why?" Christian tradition answers with an equally insistent clarity, "I don't know. But it will." It is not the greatness of our accomplishments that God values, it is the sincerity of our efforts. Accomplishments are God's concern. Effort is ours.

Eighteenth Sunday
in Ordinary Time

This Gospel passage that we have just heard is another in a five- or six-week-long series of readings all taken from the sixth chapter of John's Gospel. Taken together, these readings give us a picture of Christ's attempt, for the first time, really, to introduce to his followers the idea of the Eucharist.

But before he could do that, there would have to be a good deal of preparation. So Christ calls back to the minds of the people instances from their own history in which God revealed God's nature by providing God's people with food, such as the multiplication of the loaves by the prophet Elisha in last week's first reading, the manna in the desert today, and so on.

To this the people respond, "Show us why we should follow you. Do something God-like. Feed us. Keep us comfortable and happy." In effect they are saying, "If you want to be God, fine. But be God on our terms. Then we will follow you gladly."

Here Christ has to radically alter the direction of the conversation, and of the people's understanding. He says, "Oh, I will give you bread all right. But the bread I will give you doesn't have much to do with being comfortable and full. It has to do with being alive."

The people say, "Well, that sounds pretty good. Give it to us." And Christ, "I am that Bread of Life." It is as if he is saying, "The bread I give will never make any sense to you until I do. Until you can say that a thing is true because I say it, or a thing is good because I do it, you will never be ready to take the bread of life."

You may remember that last weekend we talked a little bit about the meaningfulness of our efforts at virtue. How each of us sooner or later reaches the point at which we must ask, "Is it really worth all the trouble it takes to try and hack one's way though life in at least a halfway decent and Christian way?" Well, anything that Christ did is meaningful, valuable, purposeful, because Christ did it.

Why is there a point to being patient and forgiving over and over again in an exasperating and frustrating world? Because Christ was patient and forgiving over and over again in an exasperating and frustrating world, and Christ acts meaningfully. Every claim that Christ makes for himself, he makes for the Eucharist. Every promise that he made to those who accepted him, he makes to those who accept the Eucharist. The Bread of Life is still with us. If we do take it, and eat it in memory of him, because he did, then our lives will be purposeful, satisfying, valuable. They may not always be comfortable, those lives, but they will always be good.

Nineteenth Sunday
in Ordinary Time

Again this weekend the liturgy centers on the image of the Bread of Life, the Eucharist.

Slowly, those who heard him began to get beyond the immediacy of physical hunger for physical bread, and began to realize that what was being offered them was indeed bread from heaven, the bread of life. It is such a powerful, consistent theme in Christian revelation, really. God gives life.

The first reading pictures Elijah as running for his life through the desert. Elijah had been very public in his criticism of the reigning queen in Israel, Jezebel. For that he had been literally run out of town, under threat of death. So the reading pictures a broken man flat on his face in the desert sand, exhausted, discouraged, begging God to let him die.

But YHWH doesn't try to convince Elijah of the point of life, the value of it. Rather, YHWH simply feeds Elijah. Somewhere, I can't remember where, I read an interpretation of this scene, and I've always remembered that verse; "There is no use in crying. Some gifts I will not give. I do not deal in dying. If you love me, live."

That is an answer that is picked up by Christ in the Gospel reading. Christ claims to literally be the food, the life giving nourishment for his people. In Christ's own words, "I am the Bread of life. Those who eat my flesh and drink my blood find borne in them the ability to live fully, authentically, forever."

It is at this point in the Gospels, with statements such as this, that puzzlement, suspicion, become active hostility. The word that is used here is one that in the original language does not admit of a symbolic or abstract interpretation. He meant "eat."

More than that, it was part of Hebrew tradition that manna, bread from heaven, would be given again, and when it was, it would be a sign of the Day of the Lord, when Israel would be returned to the glory of David and Solomon. But Christ told them that the glory of David and Solomon simply is not what it means to be alive. He told them, rather, that to be alive means to do what I do, be what I am. The virtues, the qualities of life are those underlined in the second reading, from Paul's letter to the Ephesians: kindness, compassion, mutual forgiveness, emptied of bitterness and anger, harsh words, malice of any kind.

So, to the extent that all of that actually is a portrait of each of us, we take the Eucharist as it is offered, as the bread of life. For us, as for Elijah, the message of the angel is the same. "Get up and eat, you have a long way to go. Take what is offered. It will be enough. If you love me, live."

Twentieth Sunday in Ordinary Time

This reading is another in a series of passages from John's Gospel in which Christ presents himself under the image of bread. His claim is clear: "Those who eat my flesh and drink my blood will have eternal life."

In the first reading, Wisdom is pictured as calling the people of God to a banquet, a table laden with rich food and choice wine. Beyond simply the life-giving effect of food, the emphasis is on the pleasure to be found there, the satisfaction of taking part in that meal. The feast that is the company of God, offered by Wisdom, isn't just sustenance, it is perfect fulfillment.

So Christ was applying to himself this other stream of imagery as well, and in doing so was claiming to offer ultimate fulfillment, perfect satisfaction to those who eat his flesh and drink his blood.

Now, if we were to take an exit poll after Mass this morning, and ask each participant here if they felt perfectly fulfilled and satisfied, I'd be willing to bet that the poll would show that our experience here falls short.

But perhaps that really underlines another dimension of the celebration of the Eucharist, the fact that the sacrament chosen by Christ as the instrument of his presence is nothing more exotic and out of the ordinary than bread. Bread, after all, is very much the stuff of daily life, and the eating of it a nourishment for the meeting of daily challenges. So by Christ's choice, the Eucharist has been placed in the midst of life, and cannot be rightly understood, truly celebrated apart from the rest of life any more than the noon meal can be rightly seen as anything other than integrally a part of the rest of whatever is yet to be done that day.

Perhaps we must leave here a little hungry, but more aware of the value of that for which we hunger. If the Eucharist satisfied our hunger for love, there would be no need to reach out to other people in an effort to build love. If the Eucharist satisfied our hunger for creativity, there would be no need in us to rebuild our world in newer, richer, better, more satisfying ways. If the Eucharist satisfied our hunger for life, there would be no need in us to counter those who deal in death, no need to comfort the sorrow, ease the pain of those around us. If the Eucharist satisfied our hunger for goodness, there would be no need in us to stir up goodness in the world around us. If the Eucharist satisfied our hunger for God, there would be no need to seek God anywhere else. Far better that we leave here hungrier than ever for those things, and more determined than ever to see that hunger satisfied. A well-done ceremony is a fine thing, but a re-created world is much more what Christ means by Eucharist.

Twenty-First Sunday
in Ordinary Time

These Scriptural readings underline for us that point at which a person has to decide whether all of the good examples, the advice, and the influence that have been offered are going to be accepted or rejected. It is that decision, really, that makes the difference in a person's life.

Those whom the Gospel today presents as the disciples were at just such a point. Until then they had listened to Christ, and Christ's words had done a lot to them. But now it was time for them to do something. By this time, Christ had told them that a truly successful, happy, meaningful human life was to be found in the practice of love of God and love of neighbor. He had told them that such a life was possible because of the relationship that he had come to establish between God and his people, a relationship that is symbolized, brought into being, in the Eucharist, which he called the bread of life, which he even called his own body.

But once he had said that, there was nothing Christ would do to force his listeners to live as he had taught. It was purely up to them to say yes or no. If they said no, as some did, then that would be the end of it. Their lives would stay pretty much as they had been. But if they said yes, their lives, and all of history, really, would change.

Such a critical point is pictured so simply, so undramatically. There are no voices from heaven. There are no thunderbolts, not even any nice flashy miracles to sort of pad the decision in Christ's favor.

But Christ didn't want to convince them; he wanted to invite them. Thunderbolts and miracles may be fine things, but they pretty well compromise a person's freedom to choose, and if that had been the setting, whatever the apostles' response might have been—be it fear, awe, obedience, whatever—it would not have been faith.

I think that same thing is true at the times during the course of our lives when we are called to respond to the invitations that Christ gives to us. Because it is always just that. An invitation. In everything that Christ asks us to do, he leaves us free. He never convinces anyone, he never forces anyone. He asks us to supply our own conviction, to limit our own freedom by the choices that we make.

A choice it is, indeed. We can say at any point in our lives, "Nobody can take this stuff seriously," and walk away. There will always be those who will do that. There will be those who simply cannot leap the chasm between being a hearer and a doer of the word; one who has simply listened to Christ, and one who follows him. Or we can say with Peter, "Lord, there is just nowhere else to go."

Twenty-Second Sunday
in Ordinary Time

In the Gospel for one of the weekday Masses not so long ago, there is a passage in which Christ is answering questions from a crowd of people, and one of the questions was, "Master, what must I do to be saved?"

What is important here is that a new answer was given to that age-old question, "What must I do to be saved? What is the right way?" And the new answer given by Christ was, "I am."

For hundreds of centuries before Christ, religious leaders had answered the question, "What is the right way?" by presenting their followers with a list of rights and wrongs, a body of laws to follow. The idea always was that if a person acted in this or that way, then that person was holy and could be sure of salvation.

The Jews of Christ's time were a good example of that. Over the centuries, they had developed an extremely complicated and rigorous body of law. Now certainly there were plenty of good reasons for most of those laws. Simple sanitation, for one. But the people had gone far beyond that, and had attached such a degree of importance to those laws that salvation itself depended on them.

But for Christians there was to be a new standard to use in judging righteousness. It was not a standard that could be put down on paper. Rather, it was a standard that could only be lodged in the heart. It was to be the action of grace, the word of God, purifying and changing and renewing us from within. In the Gospel,

Christ says that nothing outside of us can make us pure or impure, good or bad. It is what is buried deep within us that does that. It is the pride, the anger, the lust, the jealousy that we carry around inside of us that is the source of evil in the world. And no law, no ritual can eliminate that. Only the change of heart that comes from grace, from God's life in us, can do that.

Certainly Christ did not come to do away with the laws and commandments of religion. He simply said they are not nearly enough. The law, the Commandments, tells us do not kill, do not steal, honor your neighbor's marriage, and so on. Most of the time it is not so difficult to avoid all of those things. But Christ gave us the Beatitudes. He said, "Be humble . . . be just, be charitable, be merciful, be gentle, be forgiving, be respectful."

Ah, now those things are difficult. Compared to the morality of Christ, keeping the commandments is the very least that is expected of us.

So, I suppose there will always be some sort of tension between law and grace. But it is a healthy tension, a tension that prompts us not only to look outward at what we do, but inward, at what we are.

Twenty-Third Sunday
in Ordinary Time

Perhaps the most appropriate homily this morning would be to simply repeat the opening line of the first reading, "Say to those whose hearts are frightened, be strong, fear not. Here is your God. He comes to save you."

That must have been a welcome message for the people. They were a people in slavery, in exile. God's presence was certainly not an obvious thing. There was no burning bush, no bolt of lightning. There was only the quiet voice of the prophet telling them, "Don't be afraid. Whatever happens, it will not destroy you. Your lives will be great and valuable things if you accept the salvation God offers you, and accept it as God offers it, not as you might expect it to be. Do not expect to see the presence of God in things that happen to you, or around you. Rather, expect to find God in that which happens within you."

God's presence is not seen in the removal of stress, of problems, even of suffering from human life, but in the fact that in spite of all of that, there is still the possibility of great goodness, great accomplishments, great growth and the satisfaction, the fulfillment that such brings.

It always intrigues me in the miracle stories in the Gospels how Christ himself seems to downplay the significance of his healings. So often healing is followed by Christ telling the one who was cured not to say anything about it. Even more emphatically, in today's story it says that Christ took the man off by himself, away from the crowd before he cured him.

It would have been very simple for Christ to have used his power to rid the world of suffering and evil simply with a word. But to have done that would have been false to the Father's design for the salvation of the world, salvation not through power, but through choice, conversion of mind and heart. The real significance of the miracle stories is grasped, I think, when they are seen not so much as sweeping proof of divine power, but rather as personal acts of goodness, simply an instance of a human being using whatever resource he has at his disposal, to be of help to another. That is the Father's plan for salvation.

So, the only thing we really need to fear is the fact that we might fail to answer our call to growth in personal goodness. There is a great deal that each of us can do about the hungry, anxious, lonesome individual that lives right next door to us, perhaps in our own families, perhaps just a few feet away in this room this morning. And we will do it. We will miss some opportunities, surely, but we won't miss them all. We don't even really need to fear our own failure. Isaiah's words are true. Be strong. Don't be afraid. God is here.

Exaltation of the Holy Cross

This weekend we observe the feast of the Triumph of the Cross, and in doing so we focus our attention on the concrete reality of the cross in the life of a believer. The simple fact is that burdens, problems, sometimes even outright hardship, are a reality, and they are a reality for everyone.

But I think this feast urges us to get beneath the surface of our experience of hardship, whatever it might be, and see a goodness in it. In the life of a believer nothing means simply what it feels like. Everything means what Christ says it means. In the light of faith, hardship is not simply a burden. It is, in fact, a cross. Those two words really don't mean the same thing at all. The cross is a uniquely, mysteriously Christian burden. It is hardship with a point. Suffering that leads somewhere, means something.

Christ began to carry his cross the moment he decided that the value of his mission far outweighed any consideration of whether or not that mission made him popular and acceptable and powerful, or made Him an outcast, a figure to be scorned, ridiculed, and finally killed. For Christ, that was the heart of what the cross means. Fidelity. Never to sway from the course known to be the will of the Father, no matter how it may have felt at the moment.

It also means acceptance, unconditional acceptance of the human condition. Christ could have avoided that easily enough. There are hundreds of ways to hide from the woundedness of the human condition. He could have hidden himself in any number of different roles or costumes. He could have curried power, popularity, been a crowd pleaser. He could have built a wall of unconcern around himself, too thick for anyone to pierce. And had he done any of that, he would not have been arrested. He would not have died. But neither would he have healed or consoled or taught or saved.

It also means forgiveness. Perhaps there is no other way we can treat one another that more clearly reflects the way God treats us. Christ's last words were, "Father, forgive them. They don't know what they are doing." Something in us seems to say he should have gone down fighting, resisting, cursing his tormentors, rather than blessing them. If he had done that, he would have been a folk hero. People would have told stories about him around campfires—for a while. But they would not have preached his Gospel for two thousand years.

The ultimate truth about the cross is simply this: faithfulness, acceptance, forgiveness are virtues that work. I said that a cross is a burden with a point, but it is also a burden that is no longer deadly. No matter how it may seem to those watching, the truth is, the cross doesn't kill. But the only way to learn that is the truth is to pick it up and carry it.

Twenty-Fifth Sunday
in Ordinary Time

For me, and I'd imagine for most people, one of the scriptural themes that is most difficult to accept is the theme of the cross as a part of Christian living, the fact that Christ first offered himself to the world as victim, rather than presented himself as king. There seems to be something in us that demands that if we must indeed carry a cross, we should at least have character enough to do so angrily, bitterly, resisting every inch of the way. Certainly not, as the Old Testament prophet Isaiah put it, like a lamb led to the slaughter.

It is here, I think, that the notion of victimhood as a saving thing begins to become a little clearer. Christ could have refused that cross. He could have destroyed his persecutors. But he didn't. Because if Christ had accepted the terms of his persecutors, acted toward them as they did toward him, there would really have been no difference between the Savior and the persecutor, the builder and the destroyer. So perhaps Christ's victimhood lies not so much in a choice of the cross, but rather in a choice not to avoid it, not to counter it in kind. This, I think, is really the heart of it. The heart of the Christian vocation is a call to faithfully place oneself at the disposal first of the Father, and then of his creatures. And that demands that we take a very particular stance toward the good of others. It demands that we determine, as honestly as we can, what is truly good for those around us, and then do what we can to provide it, even at the expense of our own comfort.

Well, the simple fact is that if we do that, there will be a cross. Because sooner or later, we will come into contact with people who choose otherwise, people who find our attitude offensive or weak. People whose values, like the first instinct of the apostles in today's Gospel, are centered on power, control over others, rather than harmony. People who see in others not someone to love, but something to be used, people whose concern is not relationships of peace, but rather personal gain.

When we do come into contact with such people, we must choose again. We can choose either to react to them in the same way, to defend ourselves, perhaps even to do them one better, and in the process become them. Or we can choose to continue in the attitude of Christ, the stance of loving harmony. And if we do that, we may be victimized at the hands of those who don't.

But for a Christian that is nothing to fear, nothing to run from. It is simply a part of life lived faithfully. In all of its aspects, a believer accepts life, blesses it. We may not always understand it. But we always call it good.

Twenty-Sixth Sunday
in Ordinary Time

There is a cutting edge to these scriptural readings for this weekend. Certainly the words that Mark records as coming from the mouth of Christ are not gentle ones. The choices that Christ lays out for his followers in this Gospel are very black and white. Anyone who is not with me is against me. If anyone interferes with someone else's efforts to follow Christ, by scandal or bad example, it would be better for that person to be tossed into the ocean with a millstone around the neck.

Those who hold back, or hedge in their own choice of Christ's values, had better do some drastic rearranging of their lives if they hope to be saved. In imagery that is almost gruesome, Christ tells his followers, if it is your hand or your foot or your eye that leads you astray, cut if off, pluck it out.

Now the point must certainly be made that by no means was Christ literally calling for the cutting off of hands and feet and eyes. But he certainly was insisting that nothing is worth sacrificing salvation, and those foolish enough to throw away their hope of salvation in favor of anything else deserve just what they get.

There are so many tempting attachments in our lives that can seem to be so good, so satisfying, so important. Any number of times each of us must choose between those kinds of satisfactions and Christ. In this situation, I can make a pile of money, or I can be Christian and miss out on all that. In that situation I can be popular, fit in with the crowd, or I can be Christian, and perhaps really be left out, maybe even pushed out, laughed out. In another situation, I can get revenge on someone I really dislike, someone who has genuinely offended me, or I can be Christian, and perhaps even see that person get the better of me again. And on and on.

I think it is that simplicity of choice that so often is our problem. Surely God doesn't really expect me to pass up the chance at a pile of cash, when it would be such a satisfying thing to have. Surely God doesn't expect me to pass up the chance to be accepted, supported, fit in. Surely God doesn't expect me to pass up the especially delicious satisfaction of getting even with someone who has really hurt me, and more than likely will do so again given half a chance. Well, the answer to all of those is, "Yes. God does. That is exactly what God expects." God expects us to realize that such satisfactions, as James puts it in the second reading, very quickly decay, and leave those who pursue them with nothing. If we are foolish enough not to realize that, then nothing is what we shall have.

Twenty-Seventh Sunday in Ordinary Time

Mark's Gospel is a very carefully constructed piece of work, constructed to make a point, to teach coherently the nature of God and the nature of those God claims as God's people. And the point for Mark is a profound one. It is that those whom God claims as God's people is, simply enough, everyone.

Certainly, the teaching here is about marriage. But more than that is being said. The teaching here, it seems to me, is that that which God has brought any other of us is every bit as divinely ordained, every bit as infused with the Spirit, as is the marriage relationship. Time and again in the Scripture, the image of a marriage feast is used as the clearest illustration of the coming together of all of God's people in the fullness of the kingdom.

The point of Christ's response, really, is that marriage, like everything else, has changed with him. Marriage could no longer be understood as a relationship between just two people. Rather, it was to be a covenant between two people and God. The binding force in a marriage, then, is not the vows, nor even just the couple's love for each other. The binding force is rather God's own presence in that relationship. Christ didn't say what the marriage ceremony has drawn together, nor even what human love has drawn together let no one separate. Rather, God said, "What God has drawn together, let no one separate."

But again, there is a great deal more being taught here than the sacramental nature of marriage. We are invited, every one of us, to carefully examine our own lives, to measure the extent to which we really do see ourselves as drawn together by God's will with everyone who enters into our lives. Or do we also, too many times in too many ways, separate what God has joined?

There is a very simple standard that each of us can use in making that measurement: To what extent is my life marked by adversarial relationships? To what extent do I describe myself, my life, in terms of me against them or me against him or her and so on?

In our society, in our Church, even in our families, over issues of race, of economics, of power, even of gender, too often we separate what God has joined together. This Gospel reading closes with the image of Christ telling his followers that they must become like children if they wish to enter the kingdom of God. Well, certainly one of the clearest lessons to be learned from the life, the mind of a child is really the lesson of the first reading . . . how utterly dependent we are on one another. To realize that, and to rejoice in it, is to honor indeed what God has joined together.

Twenty-Eighth Sunday in Ordinary Time

The readings this weekend can lead to some very sobering reflection. In Paul's words from the second reading, "Nothing is concealed from Him, all lies bare and exposed to the eyes of Him to whom we must render an account." Moving into the company of God is like running into a two-edged sword. In Paul's very graphic, almost grim imagery, a sword that leaves us open, split apart.

And that, I think, is just about what is happening in the Gospel reading. Christ is approached by a man who asks a very common, very human question. "What do I have to do to be saved?" There is no reason to assume that this questioner was anything but a good man. He addresses Christ in the same vein, "Good teacher." It is as though he assumes a common ground with Christ.

And then the two-edged sword is drawn. Christ focuses first on an area with which his questioner would be comfortable: external behavior; keeping the rules; don't kill people, don't lie, don't steal.

But it was a reassuring focus for the questioner. It was a costume in which he could clothe himself pretty confidently. "I've done all that, ever since I was a child." And doubtless he had.

Then the heart of that exchange, a moment of genuinely divine revelation. The questioner was about to find himself in the presence of someone who saw him as God sees him. To Christ the man's weakness, his fear, his guilt were laid bare. And it just didn't matter. Far from rejecting or upbraiding the man, the Gospel says

103

that Christ looked at him with love and invited him to move in closer, to set aside the dearest of his costumes, that of a successful, wealthy man, with all the status and influence that carries with it. But, he couldn't do it. So he moved away, to where he could wear his masks and his costumes much more comfortably. He must have done so knowing that Christ was not going to chase him down. He never does. So the Gospel says he moved away sadly, knowing that something important, something divine had just happened in his life, and he had missed it.

So, a complex, demanding passage. As complex and demanding as is the life of faith. The focus in this exchange is on a very particular costume, and a dear one . . . wealth, success, comfort. But exactly the same thing can be said about skill. It could be a long list. We are, after all, skillful costume makers. And if the image of a two-edged sword cutting away those costumes is a harsh one, it is well tempered in the Gospel. After all, it was when the mask was beginning to be lowered that Christ looked on his questioner with love.

Twenty-Ninth Sunday
in Ordinary Time

This Gospel reading is a clear example of our universal call to service and ministry within the Church. Certainly there are hierarchical and sacramental functions and ministries, but these exist only against the backdrop of the broader baptismal call to ministry given to every one of us. And what a rich depth of meaning that simple truth gives to what we propose to do here this morning.

We are, each one of us, a part of a gathering, an assembly of people. It is one of the first and most profound truths of the Church. It is literally what the word "church" means. If we do not understand and embrace the truth of our assembly, then we cannot understand and live out the truth of our ministry.

But we are here more than simply this person next to that person next to that person and so on. Here the whole is greater than the sum of its parts. As we move into one another's company, we each become something more than we were. Simply the physical act of gathering here is itself already a creative act. By God's will, not by our doing, this gathering is given a new meaning, a new level of being that changes each one of us.

Then the final reality, the real meaning of the assembly will be spoken again here by all of us. It is Christ's words we will use. We will do it just as he did. We will bring into our midst a piece of bread, and we will say of it, "This is my body." As we do, the bread will change. It will be the body of Christ. We will break the bread, pass it among ourselves, and eat it. The Eucharist and the assembly will be joined as one. The assembly will become Eucharist. More indeed than what we were.

Let us, each of us, cast ourselves in an active role indeed in the midst of this assembly. Each of us here can worship with words. From the prayers of the petition, to the Our Father, to the simple amen at communion, speak them loudly, clearly. We can pray with our ears as we listen to the readings and hear not just the words, but the meaning, the power of Scripture. We can pray with our eyes as we look around at the godly beauty in the faces, the bodies, and the lives of the people with whom we gather. How right it is to remind ourselves how gentle we must be with one another. And we can pray with our hands at the greeting of peace. As you say, "Peace be with you," make it more than a hope. Make it a pledge. Pledge yourself to somehow be an agent of peace in the life of that person. To the revelation "This is the body of Christ," let our amen mean, "Yes, it is. And yes, we are."

Thirtieth Sunday in Ordinary Time

The miracle stories in Mark are good reading. They are colorful, dramatic, full of lots of human detail. But at the same time, they are very carefully structured stories, stories of the complex, step-by-step movement from non-belief to belief, and from belief to discipleship, imitation of Christ.

The Gospel passage this morning is the only story in Mark in which the person who is healed is given a name: Bartimaeus. Bartimaeus is far more than simply a passive recipient of Christ's healing power. In Bartimaeus's cry for help, he calls Christ the "Son of David," the only time in Mark's Gospel that title is used. Even before Christ's power is exercised, the man's prayer is one of faith. That title would be a clear reference to the connection between the power of Christ in the healing, and the passion of Christ in Jerusalem, the city of David.

Another detail that is recorded in no other story in Mark: of all those who are healed by Christ in Mark's Gospel, only this one got up and followed him down the road. Bartimaeus managed to get beyond his own newfound well being, his own satisfaction. He recognized and accepted the fullest implication of what had happened, of who Christ was, and he acted on that. Mark seems to be saying that he followed Christ into Jerusalem, perhaps up to the cross and beyond.

One more detail that is recorded as far as I know in no other story: when Christ heard the shouts of the blind man, the Gospel says that he stopped, ready to be of help. In other stories we might see Christ walking over to where the man was sitting, or waiting while others brought him over. But here, in this image of movement to discipleship, none of that happens. This time Christ calls to the man from a distance. "I will help you, of course," he says. "But before I do, you get up, and come over here where I am."

Bartimaeus could have responded to that, I suppose, in a couple of different ways. He could have responded with self-pity: "I can't. I am blind, I am afraid to move around. Please, you come over here and help me." And, no doubt, Christ would have. Or, Bartimaeus could have responded with anger: "What's the matter with this guy? I just told him I'm blind. He should come over here and help me." And, no doubt, Christ would have.

But Bartimaeus didn't do any of that. Instead the Gospel says he threw of his cloak, jumped up, and went over to Jesus. Perhaps stumbling, perhaps falling, perhaps just guessing where Christ was, but moving. And it was enough. He got there, and he was given sight. What a powerful image of prayer! Before he knew he could move, before there was any guarantee of success, of security, Bartimaeus got up and moved to where Christ had chosen to be.

All Soul's Day

I don't suppose there is anyone of us who would very seriously try to deny the fact that we human beings are social creatures. We were never intended by our Creator to live out our lives in a vacuum, cut off from the benefits of human companionship, and the encouragement, the support, the help that brings into our lives.

That is a truth which Christian tradition has recognized since the very beginning. That interdependence has been called the Communion of Saints, the Mystical Body, the human family. Our tradition demands of us that we take care of one another.

But there is a dimension to that interdependence that may be puzzling to many: the almost uniquely Catholic practice of praying for the dead.

Certainly the goal of each one of us is to become the best that we can be, to realize our fullest human potential as God knows that to be. Until we achieve that potential, we cannot enter the company of the Father. Salvation, after all, is a demanding thing. When the Father calls us to live with him for eternity, he calls us to set aside anything in ourselves that would make that impossible. By our own free choice, our own practice of virtue, he calls us to set about the task of purifying ourselves of any other choice, anything that might block the action of that grace. Our choice of God has to be a total thing, no reservations, no hedging, no holding back.

Well, such a total choice is no easy thing to do. It may take a
long time to get it right. It may take a lifetime. In fact, it may take
a great deal more than a lifetime. But if God is demanding, he is
also patient. As long as we are actively involved in the process of
trying to cleanse ourselves of sin, he will wait. God will never reject us or withdraw the grace of salvation, unless we reject God
and refuse that grace.

So human growth simply does not stop with death. The call
that God gives us to open ourselves to salvation does not end with
death. Nothing really important ends with death. It continues on.
Those who have died in the midst of their struggle to become perfect continue that struggle.

I have never much liked talking about souls in purgatory.
There aren't any souls in purgatory. There are people there.
Human beings, really pretty much like they always were. The
people in purgatory are still social creatures, still dependent on
other human beings for support, for encouragement. Praying for
the dead is really nothing so different from praying for the living.
It is wishing them well, giving them support, calling up the action of
God's grace in their lives. We have, after all, helped each other
through a lot of purgatory already. And we shall continue to do
so, just as long as it takes.

Dedication of the Basilica of St. John Lateran

This weekend is another of those calendar feasts that take precedence over the Sunday when they fall that way. St. John Lateran is an immense cathedral commissioned by the Emperor Constantine in the fourth century. Constantine was the Roman emperor who put an end to the persecutions and made it legal to be a Christian, following his own conversion. And he marked that conversion by commissioning the cathedral just outside the walls of Rome, up against what is called the Lateran Gate. For some thousand years before the building of St. Peter's, St. John Lateran was the papal cathedral and the center church of Christianity. It was there that the councils met, treaties were made, kings were crowned, and the course of not only Christianity, but much of Western civilization was given shape. Because of its age and rich history, St. John Lateran is still called by historians the "Mother of Christian Churches."

Now, it may be a little difficult for us, some seventeen hundred years and a half a world removed, to understand why this observance should be particularly meaningful. But there is a dimension to this observance in which we really do play a very active part. And that dimension is reflected in the fact that today, St. John Lateran is still there. For seventeen hundred years in that same spot, human beings have been celebrating love, confronting sin, and building community among themselves, and between themselves and God. To put it all in one word, for seventeen centuries people have judged that church to be a holy place.

It is a powerful thing, this sense of sacredness. And a sense of sacredness that is not at all a sort of shapeless, vaguely spiritual feeling, but rather is very much tied to the real world, the physical world, where real people live. It is experienced in terms of sight and sound and touch.

There is a word that speaks directly to that sense of sacredness. It is the word "incarnation," and it means to take on flesh and blood, to take on weight and shape and place, to give a real form to the presence of God in the midst of God's people. Long before human beings built steeples and shrines and sanctuaries, God first chose to move into the company of God's people, literally, to physically be where they are. It is most simply put: holiness is found where God has chosen to be.

That is equally true of every place in which God has chosen to be. In celebrating the dedication of St. John Lateran, we really celebrate the dedication of the world, because that is where God has chosen to be. The presence of God is as inescapable as is the presence of God's creation, and we move in the company of holiness when we move in the company of God's people.

Thirty-Third Sunday
in Ordinary Time

This is a transitional time in the Church year, these last few weeks of the liturgical calendar. It's as though everything there is to say has already been said, and soon the final seal will be placed on the feast of Christ the King. And the Sunday after that we will begin again the powerful, reflective, grace-filled season of Advent.

The readings this weekend seem to already reflect something of the Advent season. There is a sense of heightened expectation, a feeling that something wonderful, something godly is gathering force, is about to happen. As that goes on, a deepening sense of what it means to be a people of hope, a people keenly aware that what we experience now, what it feels like to simply be human, is far from all there is. The Father's design for the lives of his people is far from complete. There is a very great deal more yet to come in the life of each one of us. But that great deal more will not be of our own making. It is, after all, the Father's design, and it will be brought to completion on his terms, in his time. So to the notion of hope is added that of waiting. In Christ's own words in this Gospel reading, the day and the hour when all of this is to take place is not ours to know. Enough to know that it will, and for that, to wait in hope.

That final fullness of the Father's design is a theme which fires our imaginations as much as it did that of the scriptural authors. The Day of the Lord, the end times, the end of the world. It is described in Scripture in any number of different places, using a wealth of imagery. Sometimes the images are of great power, irresistible, even destructive power, such as those in the Gospel. Sometimes the images are military, such as the first reading, the return of the Lord pictured as the entrance of a victorious general into a conquered city. Sometimes the images are agricultural, such as the parables in Matthew picturing the final gathering into the barn of the final harvest. In St. Paul, the image is one of new birth, a new humankind right now growing within us, struggling to be born. In St. John the imagery is more often one of the new Jerusalem, a new and perfect society, human beings in perfect relationship to one another and to God. So a wealth of images, all of them true, none of them true enough.

So, for now, a few more days of quiet, of looking back at the year of salvation just passed. But for God's people, that quiet is never a matter of simply ending something. It is always in preparation for something new and powerful about to begin. For God's people, there is always more to come.

Christ the King

This weekend we mark the closing of the liturgical year. So it is that this weekend the liturgy attempts to present us with an image that somehow sort of sums up all that has been said.

In the first reading, Daniel is recording his vision of Christ, centuries before Christ was born. He speaks of the Son of God who approaches the throne of the Ancient One, a Hebrew title for God, and receives from God dominion over all creation.

In the second reading, John uses Christ's own words, "I am the Alpha and the Omega, the beginning and the end. The One Who is, and Who was, and Who is to come . . . the Almighty." In this there is a clear echo of the very first thing that God revealed to God's people when he told his name to Moses, "My name is Yahweh, the One Who is, Who continues to be."

To reveal the truth of God's relentless existence, and the effect that it must have on human understanding, the scriptural authors use the image of royalty. The victim, the shepherd, the prophet, the redeemer, the teacher, is ultimately the Lord, Christ the King.

Probably, at the time these passages were written, it was easier for people to relate to the image of a king than it is for us today. But perhaps that helps to underscore the real nature of Christ's kingship. From the Gospel, "My Kingdom is not of this world." Christ is not like other kings. All of the usual trappings of power, all the things on which rulers depend to maintain their authority, wealth, fear, control, even violence, none of these have anything to do with building the kingdom of God, and none of these are worth anything at all in a person's attempt to find a place in that kingdom.

But even though it is true that the kingdom of God is not yet to be found very fully realized in our earthly institutions and societies, that really should not be discouraging. After all, we have been told that that is not where we should expect to find it. The kingdom, Christ said, is begun with you. The fact that it is difficult to see doesn't mean that it doesn't exist. It does indeed exist, and it continues to grow in the efforts of millions of virtuous people who selflessly shoulder the burdens and responsibilities of a very imperfect world, people who seek out and recognize the truth, and translate that truth into virtuous lives, regardless of how out of step that may make them seem in the eyes of the rest of the world.

From the first moment of created time, till the last moment of time, and on into eternity, the Alpha and the Omega, the renewing presence of Christ gives shape and direction to everything we must do and be. The reign of Christ is the ultimate truth. It is the final fact of our lives.